Glenn Rawson STORIES

2020 - 2021 COLLECTION

GlennRawsonStories.com

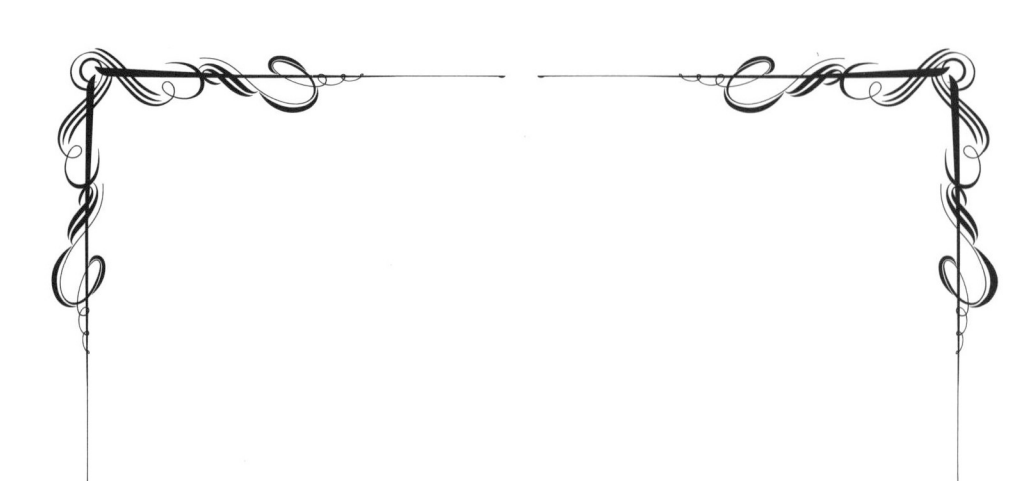

©2021 Glenn J. Rawson

All Rights Reserved. No part of this book may be reproduced in any form or by any means without permission from the author. Requests for permission may be made by contacting the author at GlennRawsonStories.com. The views expressed herein are the responsibility of the author, and do not necessarily represent the position of The Church of Jesus Christ of Latter-day Saints.

ISBN 978-1-63901-094-3

Printed in the United States of America

10 9 8 7 6 5 4 3 2

Table Of Contents

PROLOGUE vii
FOREWARD ix
1. ARE YOU A MORMON? 1
2. THE GATE 5
3. MICKEY AND GYPSY 9
4. HE WAS GONE 13
5. REBECCA WINTERS 17
6. BROTHERS CAN NEVER BE BURDENS 21
7. MY MIND IS MINE 25
8. CHOCOLATE: THE FOOD OF THE GODS 29
9. NOTHING SHORT OF A MIRACLE: THE SS ARIZONA ...33
10. TWO OLD WARRIORS MEET AGAIN 37
11. THE LORD MOVES IN MYSTERIOUS WAYS 41
12. HE PUT ME ON MY KNEES 45
13. WILLIAM FOWLER OF SHEFFIELD 49
14. I HAVE NEVER MOURNED ONE MOMENT SINCE 53
15. THE MISSION OF MERCY 57
16. THE MIRACLE OF THE LOAF OF BREAD 61
17. EZRA THAYER AND THE BOOK OF MORMON 65
18. SUCH A GREAT SACRIFICE 69
19. I HAVE BEEN PRAYING FOR YOU TO COME 73
20. THE POWER OF SACRED MUSIC 77
21. IT IS WELL WITH MY SOUL 81
22. BROTHER JOSEPH GAVE ME HIS HAND 85
23. DADDY, HELP! 89
24. A COHORT OF ANGELS 93
25. CHRISTMAS AND JOHN THE BAPTIST 97

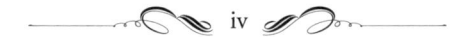

26.	ALMOST AN ANGEL	101
27.	GEORGE, DO YOU KNOW ME?	105
28.	STORM ON THE GOLCONDA	109
29.	FRARY PEAK NEW YEARS	113
30.	THE CRAZY FLICKER	117
31.	THE FORGOTTEN MISSIONARY	121
32.	MOTHERING UP!	125
33.	HE WAS SO KIND AND NICE	129
34.	CAN YOU SEE WHAT I JUST DID TO YOU	133
35.	THE TEAM WOULD NOT MOVE	137
36.	THE WANDERER	141
37.	DADDY, I'M SCARED	145
38.	MARCH 26, 1830	149
39.	THE POWER OF IPOD	153
40.	LIVING ORACLES	157
41.	SOMETHING IS GOING ON - THE GATHERING	161
42.	ADAM'S DREAM	167
43.	THE EGG ON THE HIGHWAY	169
44.	AMASA MASON LYMAN	173
45.	CHORES	177
46.	OLE AND MARN	181
47.	JOSEPH AND EMMA, THE REUNION	185
48.	THE BLIND CARVER	191
49.	THE STRANGER ON THE ROAD	193
50.	THE PLOWBOY COMPOSER	197
51.	LORD, IF THOU WILT	201
52.	GONE IN A SINGLE MORNING	205
ABOUT THE AUTHOR		209

Prologue

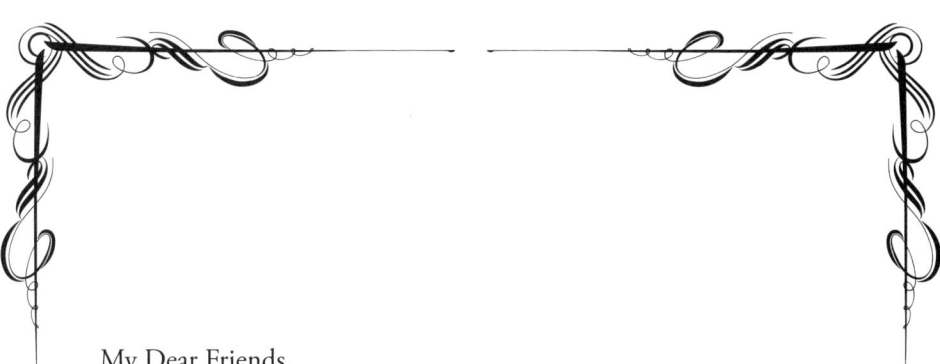

My Dear Friends,

God must love a good story because our sacred history is full of them. Every memory we cherish seems to come with a story of some sort. Every person I have ever met who loved the Lord had an inspiring story somewhere in their experience. Even the history of our lives and this world will someday be just a story from memory.

Many of the stories shared in this collection came from special friends who contributed their experiences for the benefit of us all. It is my profound hope that these stories will not be forgotten and that they will continue to instruct and inspire long after I am gone.

My constant prayer is that the Lord may use these stories for His own purposes to teach and inspire according to His own way and in His own time.

And lastly, thank you to all those who have contributed stories and all those who have by your means supported this research.

We could not go on without you.

Glenn Rawson

Forward

When Glenn called me out of the blue two and a half years ago and asked if I'd be interested in helping him share his stories with the world, I thought it would be a fun project that could help people. I've been friends with Glenn for years and I was eager to help.

Little did I know that sharing a few stories via email would blossom into a project that has allowed us to share weekly stories with tens of thousands of people each week.

This entire book was created during the pandemic and as we've reflected on the past year, we had the realization that our efforts with Facebook LIVE Firesides and other social media channels reached more than one million people.

Thanks to our VIP members and many others who have supported us by purchasing books and other products, we were able to provide a human connection and uplifting voice throughout the pandemic.

We hoped that the stories would be able to uplift and bring hope to people, but it truly has been a miracle to watch as these stories have helped so many during one of the most trying times in our history.

The Lord's hand has been involved in our success and ability to serve others with these stories, and I am grateful that I have been able to be an instrument in His hands to help Glenn share his stories and talent with the world.

I hope that when we look back in 5-10 years that we'll be able to see that, in a small way, we helped others better recognize God's hand in the lives of others, but more importantly, help each of us better recognize His hand and influence in our daily life.

Jason Tonioli

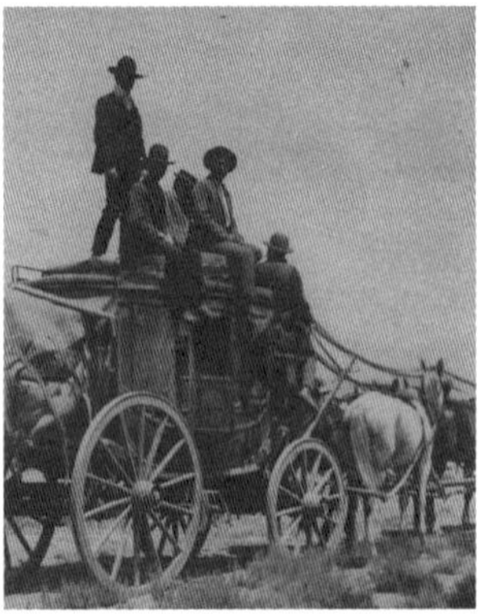

CHAPTER ONE

Are You a Mormon?

The year was 1857. Near San Bernardino, California, a young man, recently released from missionary service, was returning home to Utah. He had taken passage with a mail carrier and another man. They journeyed through the night and in the morning, stopped for breakfast near a ranch. While the other two men began cooking breakfast, the young missionary went to tend to the horses.

Just then, a wagon load of drunken men came into view. They were cursing and swearing, shouting and shooting, boasting they would kill the "Mormons." Their behavior was "almost indescribable and unendurable." They were a lawless mob such as only the West could see. One of them caught sight of the camp and made his way toward it.

The mail carrier and his companion hid in the brush, but the young man, unaware, strode into view. "The ruffian was swinging his weapon and uttering the most blood-curdling oaths and threats ever heard against the "Mormons." The young man said, "I dared not run, though I trembled for fear which I dared not show. I, therefore, walked right up to the campfire and arrived there just a minute or two before the drunken desperado, who came directly toward me, and swinging his revolver in my face, with an oath cried out:

"Are you ___ _____ ____'Mormon?'"

The 19-year-old lad "looked him straight in the eyes, and answered with emphasis: 'Yes siree; dyed in the wool; true blue, through and through.'"

The man's arms dropped to his side as if paralyzed—his pistol in one hand. The tone of his voice softened into "a subdued and maudlin" tone and he said, "Well, you are the ____ ____ pleasantest man I ever met! Shake," he said and stuck out his hand. "I am glad to see a fellow stand for his convictions." Then he turned and walked away to join his companions.

That young man was Joseph F. Smith, who later became the sixth president of the Church. Where did he learn such courage? He learned from a father who faced a mob at Carthage and died for his testimony—Hyrum Smith, and from a mother who defied all odds, opposition, and adversity to keep her family together, bring them west, follow the prophets, and build her own mountain homestead of faith—Mary Fielding Smith. Courage is that quality that drives us to stand up, face our fears, and press forward.

Source:

Gospel Doctrine: The Sermons and Writings of Joseph F. Smith, Deseret Book, 1909 p. 531-32

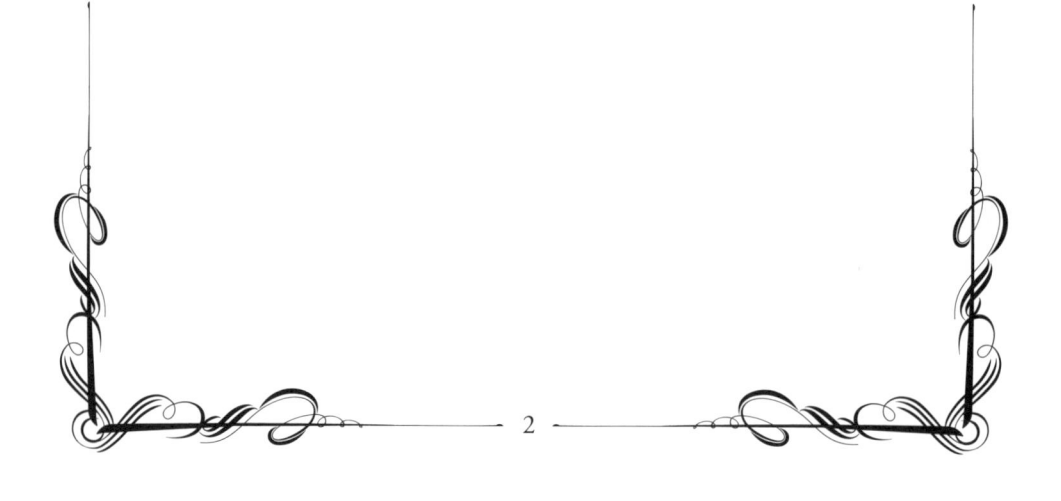

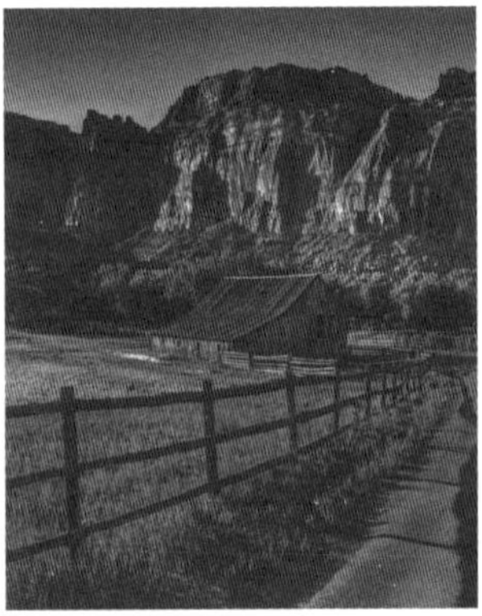

CHAPTER TWO

The Gate

It was early summer, 1916, near Tabiona in eastern Utah. The ward Relief Society president, Esther Wagstaff, decided she wanted to pay a visit to those sisters who lived across the river who had been shut in by winter snows and bad roads. She asked one of her counselors to go with her, Elena Dorothy Lambert Michie. The two of them climbed in the wagon and began their ministering journey of love and duty.

As the day progressed, they traveled from sister to sister making their visits. Each time they came to a gate to someone's property, Sister Michie would climb down, open it, wait for Sister Wagstaff to drive the wagon through, and then she would close it and climb back up in the wagon. Now, for a pioneer woman in her sixties, that's a chore, especially for one suffering from severe varicose veins. Elena or 'Grandma Lena' as her family referred to her, said,

"Well, we turned homeward, and of course, there were the gates to go through again, but we didn't talk of that. I just climbed out of the wagon and opened each gate as we came to it, and when Sister Wagstaff had driven through I closed the gate again and got back into the wagon. As we neared the last gate Sister Wagstaff said, "Hasn't this been a satisfying day? It has been so good to visit these sisters."

I said, "Yes, it's been a wonderful day. Now if we just didn't have to open any more gates!"

To our amazement, the gate just ahead of us opened by itself. The heavy piece of two by four that went from the gate into the gate posts moved by itself and the gate swung open. I had dragged it open a few hours before. Sister Wagstaff drove through. One of us said in a whisper, "Let's watch and see if it closes." We both turned around and watched as the gate swung shut and was fastened.

I just can't tell you how we felt. I guess it was a miracle right before our eyes. Those gates were heavy. You know how they were made, poles and two by fours and barbed wire. Well, we had done the best we could to do our duty. Maybe our guardian angels were there to help. I just don't know.

The Lord once said, "I will go before your face. I will be on your right hand and on your left, and my Spirit shall be in your hearts, and mine angels round about you to bear you up." (Doctrine and Covenants 84:88) And so they are!

Source:

https://www.familysearch.org/tree/person/memories/KWCF-4V5

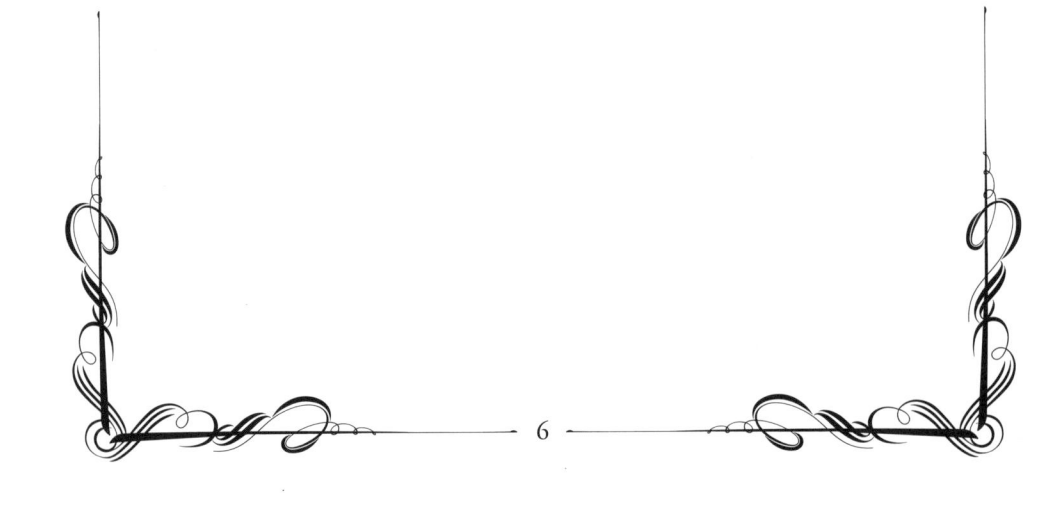

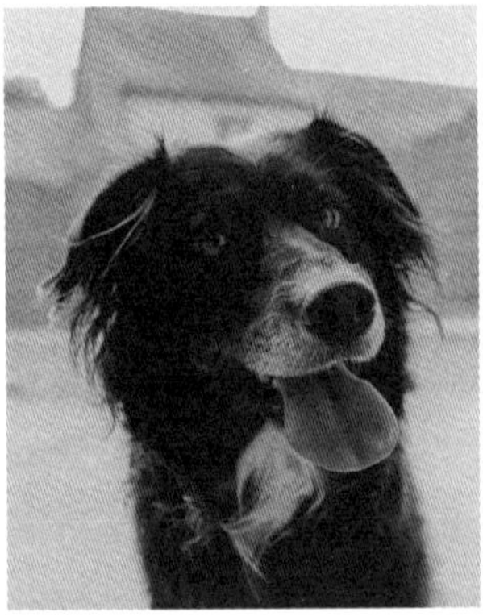

CHAPTER THREE

Mickey and Gypsy

It was the summer of 1912, near Tabiona, Utah, when Rula Michie Wrigley, who was 8 or 9 at the time, wanted to go and visit a girlfriend who lived about two miles away. Rula was given permission and told to be home by dark.

The two little girls crossed the river and decided to climb a rock hill. It was evidently so much fun that they lost all track of time. Suddenly, they noticed that the sun was not only setting but it was descending into black clouds. By the time they reached level ground, it was dark and the black clouds covered the sky.

Ella became frightened and ran for home, leaving Rula alone. Crying and scared, Rula started running for home with "only occasional flashes of lightning to show [her] way." She ran into some rocks and "fell sprawling." When she stood up, she "had lost all sense of direction." "I hadn't the faintest idea which direction to go," she said. And there were no familiar landmarks anywhere.

Remembering what her mother had taught her about prayer, Rula knelt and asked "for help and guidance that [she] might reach home safely. When I finished my prayer," she said. "I stood up, and without any hesitation, I started walking. I still didn't know which direction I was going, but I had placed my trust in the Lord and felt that He would guide me."

As she walked along, limping, in the threatening darkness, her hand swung to her side and brushed something furry. She said, "I was petrified with fear! It wasn't uncommon for people out there to meet coyotes, wolves, bears, cougars, etc. I thought one of them was about to devour me alive. I stayed in my tracks and stood perfectly still until the lightning flashed again. When I looked down, I saw a large dog looking up into my face. What a relief that was!

The dog licked my hand and I reached over and got a good grip on the hair behind his ears. We started walking. I don't know how the dog knew where I was going, but he seemed to know. I was willing to follow him no matter where he took me. I figured there would at least be people there. He led me past a neighbor's place without even attempting to enter. I didn't see it but knew we had passed it when the dog led me into our own gate and up to the house, and we made it before the storm broke. Never was anyone more happy to reach home than I, in spite of the scolding I got for being so late."

The next morning the dog was still there. No one recognized him. He didn't come from any of the neighboring ranches.

Because of that, she named him Gypsy, and he stayed. Rula said, "He used to go with me to school about halfway, and there he'd sit and watch me until I was out of sight. When I returned at night, he'd be there waiting for me. I don't know where he spent the time in between. If I were home alone, he wouldn't let anyone approach the house. He always accompanied me if I went hiking over the hills and was a most devoted friend and companion." In time, Rula was given the nickname of Mickey. They were Mickey and Gypsy, inseparable companions. Then came the day that Rula went away to school.

Gypsy disappeared three days later, never to be seen again.

"I received help when I needed it," Rula said, "and it didn't matter whether the help came from an angel or from one of His humbler creatures, a dog."

Source:

Story provided by Dallin Wrigley.

https://www.familysearch.org/tree/person/memories/KWC6-14L

David Cluff

CHAPTER FOUR

He Was Gone

David Cluff had a large family and lived in Nauvoo, Illinois. He was a carpenter and a farmer and managed to prosper, but then he answered the call and served as a missionary in the eastern states.

Upon his honorable release, he returned to Nauvoo and his family with a desire to return to work in his cabinet shop, but in his absence, his carpenter tools had worn out, and given the family's present poverty, getting new ones "seemed impossible."

He was faced with a dilemma. He needed new tools to do quality work, but he had not the means to do that work to buy the new tools. He said to his wife, "Mother, I do wish I could get ahead enough to buy a set of tools."

His son, Benjamin heard that comment. A few days later, Benjamin happened to be playing in the street in front of their home. He and the other boys witnessed "a strange-looking man with a small pack on his back such as carpenters sometimes carry tools in as they go from job to job." Benjamin observed that he turned through the gate and walked into his father's shop.

Curious, Benjamin followed the man in and heard him say to his father, "Don't you want me to make you some tools?" "Yes," came the reply. "I am needing some tools very badly, but I don't know how I can pay you." The stranger responded,

"Never mind about the pay. Have you any seasoned lumber?" David Cluff pointed to some seasoned maple at the north end of the shop and the stranger went to work—for three weeks!

Benjamin said, "When this was done, he asked father if there was anything else he wished to have done. Father replied that he had fit him up in pretty good shape. Now, said father, "How can I pay you?" Now came the strangest part of the miracle, for when father asked the question, 'How can I pay you?' the stranger replied, "you can pay me the next time you see me."

The stranger then picked up his tools, bid David goodbye, and walked. Young Benjamin followed him out and stood at the gate watching him walk away. He said, "Before the stranger had gone fifty yards from the gate, my attention momentarily was drawn off, but resuming my gaze after the stranger, I was exceedingly astonished. The road was open. There was no corner, no tree, shrubs, or any other obstruction that he could secrete or hide himself behind, but he was gone from my view."

David Cluff took those tools and went to work building the Nauvoo Temple.

Source:

https://www.familysearch.org/photos/artifacts/91897002?p=2415216&returnLabel =David%20Cluff%20Sr.%20(KWJ6TK8)&returnUrl=https%3A%2F%2Fwww. familysearch.org%2Ftree%2Fperson%2Fmemories%2FKWJ6-TK8

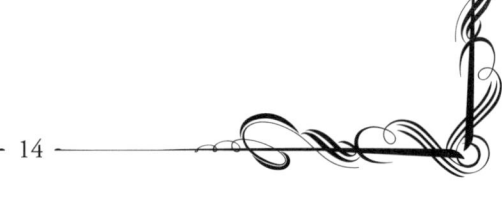

Rebecca Winters

CHAPTER FIVE

Rebecca Winters

It was the early summer of 1833, near Jamestown, New York when Rebecca Winters was given a remarkable dream. In the dream, her husband came to her and gave her a present. She could not tell what the gift was but "she realized it was something of very great value and her whole being seemed filled with light and joy that remained with her."

The next day, she pondered what the gift could be. "She could not imagine anything that he could buy for her that could cause her to feel so supremely happy."

That evening, her husband returned and handed her a book. "I will make you a present of that," he said. She looked down at the book. It was a copy of the Book of Mormon.

She had heard of this book and its origins. She opened the book and began to read, and as she did so, "her soul was filled with that same light and influence as in her dream." Her dream stood fulfilled.

Hiram and Rebecca Winters joined The Church of Jesus Christ of Latter-day Saints and faithfully followed and served wherever the saints went.

The story would be powerful enough even if it ended there—it does not.

Hiram and Rebecca Winters were among the last to leave Nauvoo, being driven out by mobs in the fall of 1846.

They worked hard to gather the means to go west with the saints. Finally, by the spring of 1852, they were ready to leave. They crossed the Missouri River and started across the plains, but in western Nebraska, cholera struck the camp, and many were taken down by it. Among them—Rebecca Winters.

It was about noon, August 15, 1852, when, despite the best efforts of many to save her, that Rebecca Winters passed away. Her loss was felt deeply in the camp and so her grave was dug unusually deep to protect it.

They tenderly dressed her, placed her on a bed, and lowered the bed. Nearby were the ruins of an emigrant wagon. Desiring that the final resting place of this good woman not be lost, they took a piece of wheel iron, bent it, and placed it in the grave. When the grave was filled in, the iron could not be pulled up. Then William Reynolds took a cold chisel and engraved her name and memory into the iron. Upon seeing it, Hiram Winters exclaimed, "That name will remain there forever."

Zebedee Coltrin would later say of Rebecca Winters, "If ever there was a good woman who lived on the earth, Sister Rebecca Winters was one."

The company moved on. The grave was lost and forgotten—that is—until the railroad was laying a line and ran into it, at the beginning of the 20th century. Out of respect, the line was rerouted and the grave spared. The grave and its marker are still there—a monument to Rebecca and the pioneers of the 19th century.

I've been to her grave several times and always feel a spirit of reverence and respect. To me, she is more than a pioneer. She represents all those of you who give your lives to the Savior and follow Him to the best of your ability. No matter what happens and when, the world may forget you and your service, but He does not and never will.

Source:

http://mormonhistoricsites.org/rebecca-winters-gravesite/

https://newspapers.lib.utah.edu/details?id=2423529#t_2423529

Hatch Family

CHAPTER SIX

Brothers Can Never Be Burdens

It was late June of 1846, in Mt. Pisgah, Iowa. Captain James Allen of the United States Army went among the refugees, seeking volunteers to join the Army in the war with Mexico. Those refugees were members of The Church of Jesus Christ of Latter-day Saints. After considerable encouragement from President Brigham Young, more than 500 men volunteered to form the first and only U.S. military battalion organized by religious affiliation.

Among those who signed up was Meltiar Hatch. He asked that his younger brother, Orin, also be allowed to join. Orin was only sixteen years of age. Family tradition holds that his father charged Meltiar to "bring him back safely." Permission was granted and the two brothers, with the rest of the volunteers, left Council Bluffs, Iowa in July 1846.

It would be an extremely difficult march of more than 2000 miles from Fort Leavenworth, Kansas to San Diego, California. In addition to long forced marches, there would be days without water, hot desert conditions, blowing sand, rugged mountain crossings, disease, and starvation. For five months, the men marched, blazing roads and trails as they went.

As their commanding officer, Colonel Philip St. George Cooke would later declare, "History may be searched in vain for an equal march of infantry."

According to Meltiar's journal and the family history, somewhere in Arizona or California, young Orin became ill and weakened to the point that he could not walk without help. Meltiar and a friend lifted him up and with one on each side, supported him. They walked on.

This continued day after day until Orin became so weak and slow that, even with help, he could not keep up. Finally, the order came that he must be left by the side of the trail to die. The company moved on without him. That night, however, after the Battalion camped, Meltiar and a friend went back, found Orin, picked him up, and brought him into camp, arriving just before the company was to depart. As the Battalion moved out that morning, once again, Orin was left behind. And again, that night, Meltiar and his faithful friend went back for Orin.

This went on day after day, until finally, their commanding officer, seeing their determination and loyalty for a brother, gave up his horse. Orin was strapped to the back of the horse and could now keep up.

When the Battalion arrived in San Diego in January 1847, Orin Hatch was with them, thanks to the love and loyalty of a brother and a friend. In fact, the family history records that he was among a group of five soldiers selected to go into the woods and cut the pole used to hoist the first American flag flown over California. It has been well-said, "Brothers can never be burdens."

Source:

https://www.familysearch.org/tree/person/memories/KWN2-8R6

https://www.familysearch.org/tree/person/memories/KWNK-QCV

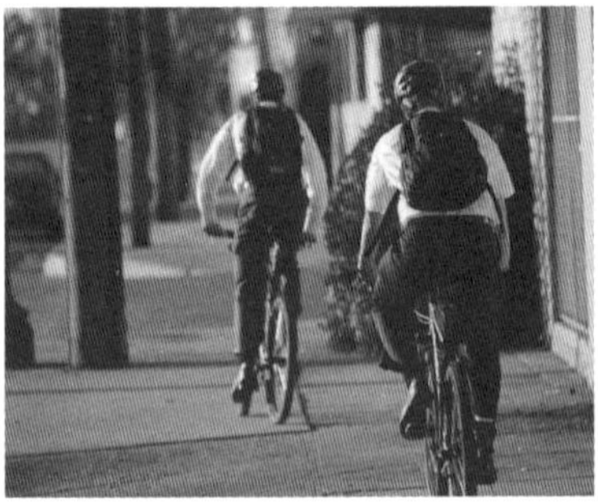

CHAPTER SEVEN

My Mind is Mine

Late one evening, many years ago, a friend and I were returning from an appointment riding bicycles. In order to get where we were going, we had to cross the oncoming lanes of traffic on a busy street. I could see a car coming up ahead, but I had plenty of time. I made the left-hand turn – no problem. But my friend was too close to the oncoming car to make the turn, but he did it anyway. He sped up and darted across in front of the car.

As he's doing these death-defying shenanigans, I was looking back over my shoulder, watching and holding my breath—still pedaling my bike. I thought for a moment he was going to be a hood ornament with a suit and a smile, but – he made it.

However, when I looked back around to the front, my bike had drifted up against the curb. Oh no! I knew what was going to happen. With all my willpower I wanted that bike to go back out in the street where it was safe. But in my panic, all I could stare at was that 'big ugly curb' that was going to get me.

Well, it got me! The bike hit the curb and went out from under me. I flew through the air landing on my back and sliding in the slimy wet green grass. My freshly cleaned suit was a mess, and my pride was worse.

I learned from that experience and others like it that wherever I'm looking, that is where my bike, my car, my body, or my life will go. Please consider— what I see is generally what I think— what I think is generally what I do. If my mind and my heart, my ears, and my eyes are constantly filled with and focused on the distracting and destructive things of this world, is it any wonder that I'm continually crashing, and my life is a mess? It is a powerful true principle—applicable in all areas of your life and mine--my mind is mine and if I make my mind mind me, my destiny is mine.

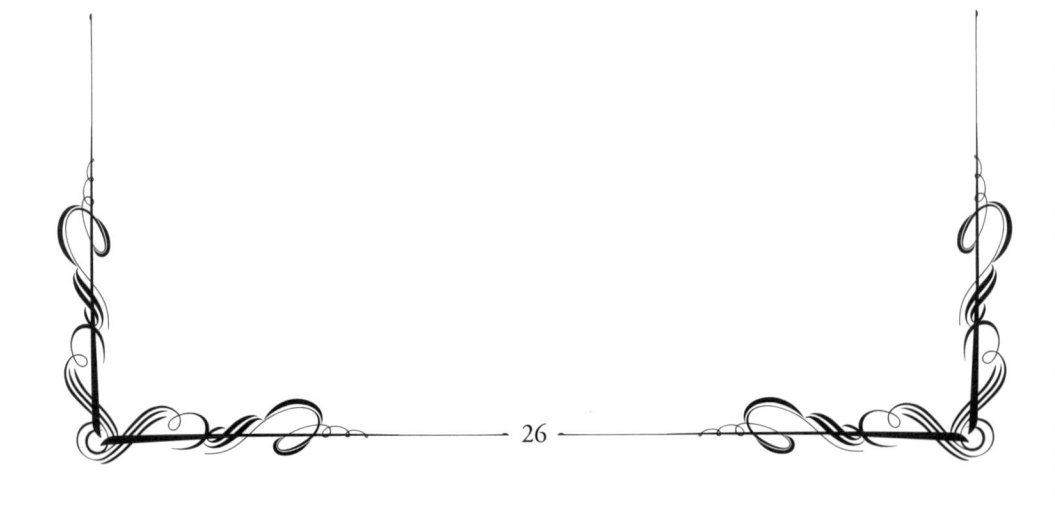

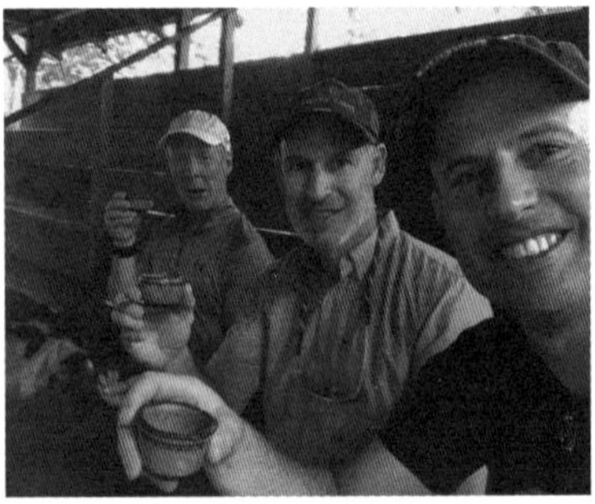

CHAPTER EIGHT

Chocolate: The Food of the Gods

Sarapiqui, Costa Rica, February 27, 2020. I was on a fascinating expedition with friends, to learn the origins of one of the most meaningful things in my life--chocolate! Since I can remember, I have loved chocolate.

I learned that chocolate began with the ancient Mayans and was considered the drink of the Gods. Only the elite could partake of it and if a single drop was spilled in the frothing process, you could be killed for sacrilege. When the Spanish came, they tasted the gritty brown liquid and didn't like it but when someone came up with the idea of adding sugar and other flavors, suddenly it was a hit and was taken back to Europe.

How those ancients ever found chocolate will forever remain a mystery. It starts with the large yellowish fruit of the cacao plant. When the fruit is just right, you break it open and there is at the center a bunch of white, juicy, fleshy beans. I popped some of those beans in my mouth and they were sweet and stringy, but if you bit into one of those beans—it was no longer sweet, but bitter and disgusting. The raw beans are then dried in the sun and then roasted. After that, they are ground up. The chaff of the hulls is then blown away leaving the brown powder which smells like chocolate, but, trust me, it doesn't taste like sweet chocolate. It is raw cocoa. The ancients would then mix it with water and boil it. It was then frothed by pouring it back and forth to add air and flavor.

Ingredients were added to enhance the flavor and you had the drink of the gods. The shaman would even add hallucinogenic herbs in order to have spiritual revelatory experiences.

Chopa, our jungle chocolatier, showed us the entire process. I tasted it at every step, but when he took the frothed chocolate and added 30% sugar and cooked it on his outdoor wood burning stove— it was to die for. It was the best dark chocolate I have ever had.

What totally intrigued me is that cacao in its natural state is nothing. You wouldn't know at first glance that something wonderful lies at its heart. The good is three layers down in the center of the fruit, and the process of finding, preparing, and refining the bitter distasteful brown powder into an international delicacy is a coveted art.

In the days since, I have pondered what I saw. People are like chocolate. In our mortal, earthly jungle state we are not much to look at on the outside but let the Almighty—the Master—take us in hand and he will find the good within and refine us until we are fit for the Gods—literally!

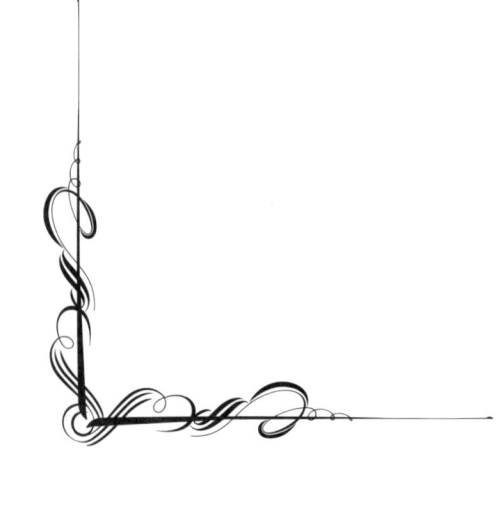

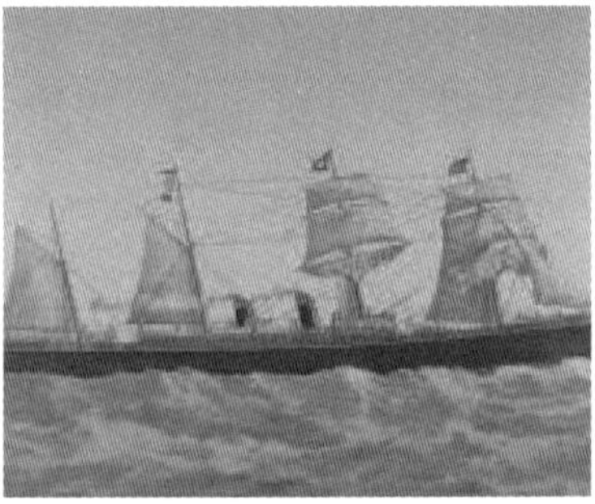

CHAPTER NINE

Nothing Short of a Miracle: the SS Arizona

November 7, 1879, about 250 miles off the coast of Newfoundland in the North Atlantic. At 8:45 p.m., four missionaries of The Church of Jesus Christ of Latter-day Saints, bound for Liverpool, were just attending to their evening prayers when the ship's engines suddenly stopped. Moments later, "a great crunching noise of crumbling timbers and sheet metal rang through the cold, clear night."

Thinking that they had collided with another ship, they ran out on deck. To their horror, they saw a mountain of ice looming above the bow of the ship. Elder Henry Aldous Dixon said, "It was a clear night and the iceberg looked similar to a bluish-white cloud looming up about 50 feet - An awful, grand sight."

Tons of ice were piled on the forecastle deck of the ship, which had been traveling at 16 knots at point of impact. When Elder John Lee Jones inspected the damage, he reported that "the force of the collision was so great as to cave in completely the ship's bow and to break off and pile up more than 20 tons of ice on top of the deck. Both anchors were severed. The huge hole in the bow, 30 feet deep by 20 feet wide, extended below the water mark; and the break extended along the whole length of the keel."

Water began to fill the ship and sailors were injured and buried under the ice. Elder Jones said, "To all appearances, we were to have a watery grave in the middle of the Atlantic Ocean."

There was pandemonium among the passengers. Elder Dixon records, "I called the boys together during the excitement and prayed the Lord to enable us to avert calamity, that it might be no worse. We exercised our priesthood, prayed for a calm, and that we might live."

They prayed for the captain and crew to have the wisdom and skill to save the ship and passengers. All luggage was ordered to the rear of the vessel and bales of cotton were stacked in the bow to slow down the flow. The ship turned towards St. Johns, Newfoundland, 250 miles away and proceeded at a speed of 8-9 knots. The only way this would work is if the ship could sail perfectly calm waters. Elder Dixon continued, "Went below to our cabins, prayed frequently according to the order of the priesthood, for a calm sea and no wind, as this is apparently our salvation temporarily."

At one point during the night, Elder Dixon says, "We went on deck and while alone, rebuked the winds and waves. We have a calm sea. Prayers answered…. Committed ourselves to God."

Moved by the Spirit of the Lord, Elder Dixon promised the passengers that "no lives should be lost or ship either, in the name of the Lord."

Thirty-six hours later, the ship limped into St. John's Harbor, passengers, crew, and ship all safe. The Captain and crew considered it, "nothing short of a miracle."

Incidentally, during the night, the owner of the ship was informed of the accident. He immediately asked if there were any Mormon missionaries aboard. When he was told, 'Yes, there are four of them,' "he then informed those around him that he knew the vessel would land safely and that they were to have no further worries or fears. His steamship line had carried Mormons for 30 years and had never lost a ship on which missionaries were passengers. Carrying Mormon missionaries was the best insurance he could buy, Mr. Guion said, and with that remark, he returned to his bed to sleep."

Source:

https://saintsbysea.lib.byu.edu/mii/account/80

Clarence D. Taylor, reprinted from the January 1963 Instructor.

https://catalog.churchofjesuschrist.org/assets?id=7b5d68a8-8c7d-46a2-9997-507f6f888e0d&crate=0&index=0

Story contributed by Steven Elkins

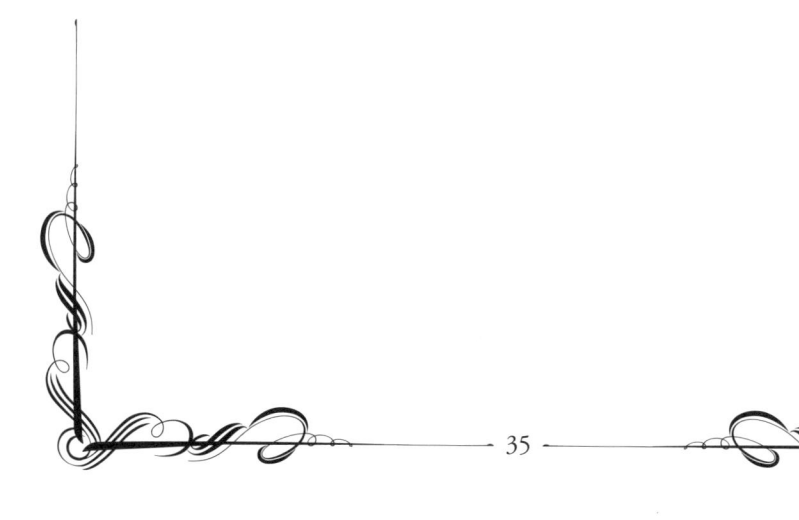

Ephraim K. Hanks

Chapter Ten

Two Old Warriors Meet Again

Allen Taylor is one of those pioneers that played a major part but has been largely forgotten by history. He joined The Church of Jesus Christ of Latter-day Saints in 1832, in Monroe County, Missouri. When the Saints were driven from Missouri by angry mobs, Allen suffered with them.

He was there again at the brutal fall of Far West in 1838. When the Church was driven from Nauvoo in 1846, Allen Taylor was among the first to leave, and when the poor were driven from Nauvoo that fall, he was called to go back across Iowa to their rescue.

At Winter Quarters, Nebraska he volunteered to join the Mormon Battalion, but was asked to remain behind and assist in caring for the poor. He came out of Winter Quarters with Brigham Young in 1848, serving as a captain. He was a true and faithful servant of the Lord, given many heavy assignments by the brethren.

Eventually, he brought his family to the Valley and became bishop in Kaysville or Kay's Ward as it was known at the time. Then, in 1861, he was called to settle Utah's Dixie- a most challenging assignment. He served there until 1883, whereupon he was released and moved to Loa, Paiute County, Utah.

There in Loa in 1884, Allen Taylor, now seventy years old, attended a church meeting in which he was called upon to speak, but as he began, he was suddenly interrupted by another aged veteran in the congregation, who asked, "Do you remember me catching a buffalo for you?"… Allen looked square into his face and asked, "What is your name?" To which the other man said simply, "Hanks." It was Ephraim K. Hanks.

"Why, Brother Hanks, how are ye?" The two advanced and indulged in a hearty handshaking. Elder Taylor then related that one evening, as he and his company were encamped on the Plains, Brother Hanks came into the camp and said there were some buffalo just around or over a little hill and thought he could get one. [Hanks] took down his lasso and started leisurely out to try. In a little while, he returned, bringing, with lasso hitched to the horn of the saddle, a fine yearling buffalo, which was brought right into camp to be butchered. The meeting of the two old friends thus, after a separation of nearly a quarter of a century, although a little comical, was very affecting."

"Allen Taylor died at the age of seventy-seven in Loa on 5 December 1891 …. As he had lived, so he died, full of faith in the work to which the greater part of his life had been devoted." His obituary concludes, "Though he had long since faded from the prominent role he once assumed, he should be remembered as one of the most important leaders in the early days of Mormon emigration."

As we grow older and our strength and energy wane, some of the old warriors among us, male and female, wonder if they have done any good in this world and will their service be remembered. It is my conviction, when all is said and done and our family histories are perfected, no good is gone from the record—your righteous service will be remembered by God and family forever.

Source:

https://www.familysearch.org/photos/artifacts/99572664?cid=mem_email

Story contributed by Carol Taylor of Carson City, Nevada, July 2020

Alois

CHAPTER ELEVEN

The Lord Moves In Mysterious Ways

Clara Metzger was born on August 15, 1886, in Rengerhausen, Germany, the seventh child in a very religious family. So devout was her family that Clara's father often assisted the Priest in church affairs. Clara grew up with the same devotion, even considering for a time becoming a nun. In time, she went to work learning the trade of a cook.

It was during that time she met a young man, Alois Hollingshaus. At first, she was not very impressed with the young postal worker because he showed no interest in her church. She informed him that she would not marry any man that did not practice as she did. Suddenly, he started going to church and became quite active. The relationship continued and they set a date to be married.

Meanwhile, Clara loved to read and read many of the books in the large library of the home where she worked. In time, she had read many of the volumes and wanted something different. Sophie Krierly was a vendor who regularly brought eggs and vegetables to the home. Clara asked Sophie if she had any books Clara could read. Sophie asked if she liked to read history. Clara responded that she loved to read histories. Without any introduction or explanation whatsoever, Sophie handed Clara a copy of the Book of Mormon.

Clara began reading it and "could hardly put it down. As she read the book, "such a feeling came over her." And even though it was hard for her to understand, she felt compelled to finish it. She waited anxiously for the day when Sophie would return.

"Well, how did you like the book?" asked Sophie.

"Oh, I loved it," answered Clara, "but the book isn't complete. There must be another book to go along with it."

"I can't bring you another book," Sophie said, "but I can take you to where you can learn about it."

Clara began meeting with the missionaries and came to know that the message of the restored gospel "was true with every fiber of her body and soul." She was baptized in icy waters on December 10, 1910.

What was she going to do now? How could she tell Alois that now she could not marry him unless he became a member of The Church of Jesus Christ of Latter-day Saints? She decided she couldn't, but the wedding day was drawing nearer. What to do…?

She concluded that she would run away. She bought a ticket to London and began packing her bags to leave. As she was packing, there came a knock at the door and when she opened it, there stood Alois. The two of them had a regularly scheduled date night and this was not it.

"What are you doing here?" she asked.

Alois explained that he was not going to be able to make their date night as he had a meeting to attend, and he named the place where the meeting was being held. Clara knew that place.

"Why would you want to go there?" she asked. "That's where the Mormons meet, and they are baptizing that night!"

We can only imagine her stunned surprise when he announced "That is why I'm going. I know the Mormons meet there, and I am going to be baptized by the missionaries."

And again, imagine the joy Alois felt to learn that his beloved was already a member of the Church. Alois was baptized on April 22, 1911, and he and Clara were married on May 3, 1911. Both Alois and Clara were bitterly disinherited and angrily disowned by their families.

In 1912, they came to Utah, and in 1913, were sealed in the Salt Lake Temple, thus beginning a remarkable life of temple service, doing the work for thousands of their kindred dead.

Indeed, the Lord moves in mysterious ways his wonders to perform!

Source:

https://www.familysearch.org/tree/person/memories/KWC6-VCS

Story contributed by Mary Ann Kirk

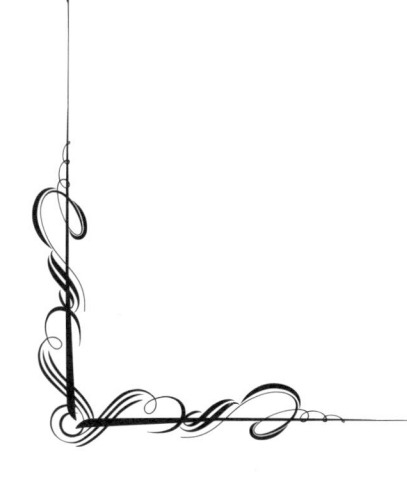

Orrin Orlando Barrys

CHAPTER TWELVE

He Put Me On My Knees

April 1878, just north of Grantsville, Utah. Young Orrin Orlando Barrys and his older brother were driving a large herd of cattle to fresh grazing. As the stock attempted to cross an alkali swamp, they became mired down in the mud. The swamp was about 100 yards across. The animals struggled, but could not extricate themselves, and the boys were powerless to help them. Finally, Orlando's brother took off for town to get help.

"I was left to stand guard over the herd and await his coming," Orlando said. "While performing this service, I became somewhat excited, seeing several of our most valuable animals struggling and plunging in the swamp. They sunk deeper and deeper into the quicksand and mire until only the heads of some of them could be seen, the rest of their bodies having sunken out of sight."

Desperately, Orlando wondered what to do. It was at that moment that he remembered his mother teaching him that when he was in trouble and needed help, he should pray.

"I raised my hand and arm to the square," he said, "as I had seen our brethren do in opening a meeting, stood up and removed my hat, and earnestly implored my Heavenly Father to take our animals out of the predicament they had gotten themselves into. No sooner had I offered this prayer than some power put me on my knees and a voice seemed to say, "Pray again". This I did more earnestly than before, if possible, asking the Lord to get the cows out of the mire as quickly as he possibly could. I had an assurance right then and there that it would be done."

At the conclusion of the prayer, Orlando ran to the top of a sand knoll and looked to see if his brother was coming. Not far away, he spied his brother and two of his uncles returning with a large span of horses and chains to drag the cattle free.

Orlando continued, "With them, I returned to the spot where the struggle was going on, when to the great astonishment of my brother and uncles, all of the aforesaid animals were completely out of the swamp. They were peacefully grazing on the green grass of the next sand knoll, and so covered with mud that they all seemed the same color (black)."

How did the animals get free? Orlando's uncles laughed and accused the boys of crying wolf, but it was evident that something extraordinary had happened- but what?

"I knew," he said, "but I was afraid to tell them how it happened, for fear they would doubt and would laugh, and would treat a sacred thing lightly. I knew that the Lord had answered my prayer and had taken the cattle out of the mire. Just how it was done, I did not know, but we saw someone leaving the swamp, as we came on the scene, riding a large horse or mule. He was only a hundred yards or so away, but he never came to receive our thanks or to tell what he had done and I am convinced that no human could have done such a big job in such a short time. We went over where he was seen and discovered the tracks of a large shod horse or mule in the sand."

Orlando concluded, "I know as I know that I live, that God heard and answered the prayer of a little boy and that the best attitude for prayer is on the knees, for he put me on my knees when I was standing up praying, and he said to me "pray again." Just how He did it, I do not know, but I believe the man on a horse was from another world."

Source:

https://www.familysearch.org/tree/person/memories/KWCH-CRD

Story contributed by Lindy Taylor

William Fowler

CHAPTER THIRTEEN

William Fowler of Sheffield

William Fowler was born May 9, 1830, in Sydney, Australia to English parents, John and Bridget Fowler. When William was just nine-years-old, his parents moved back to Sheffield, Yorkshire, England. By the age of fourteen, both of his parents had died, leaving William and his brothers orphans.

William managed to obtain a good education. He became a talented musician and singer. He often worked evenings as an entertainer. At age 18, he was baptized into The Church of Jesus Christ of Latter-day Saints. The yearning within was fulfilled.

That very month, William was called to be a missionary at home. For four years, he obediently labored to preach the restoration, notwithstanding considerable prejudice and opposition. In fact, when his employer found out he had been baptized, William was fired.

In time, he met a young woman. They fell in love and set a date to be married. She was not a member of the Church, though she attended meetings with him, and promised she would be baptized soon. In preparation for the upcoming wedding, William rented a home and furnished it.

One day, he approached his beloved and asked, "Are you going to be baptized before our wedding? "No," she said very firmly. "Why not?" he asked anxiously. "You have told me all along you would be." "What difference does it make?"

she asked. "It makes all the difference in the world to me," he answered. "I will not marry a girl that does not belong to the Church." "Well," she said, "I'm not getting baptized to suit your whim." He said, "If you thought as much of this Church as I do, you would want to belong to it. If you will not be baptized that puts an end to our marriage plans." "You do not love me," she accused, "or you would not let that hinder us." "I do love you," he said, "very dearly, but my religion means more to me than my love for a woman, so we will not be married."

As hard as it was, William stuck to his word. "With his heart full of sorrow and anguish, he turned away and saw her no more."

Then in 1854, William met Ellen Bradshaw. She too had proven herself willing to make hard sacrifices to follow living prophets. They courted and were married on February 16, 1855. As their love and family grew, William continued his labors as a local missionary, proving himself a great benefit to the saints of England. Among his valiant contributions was his music. He wrote many hymns, articles, and poems for the saints.

Sometime in the early 1860's, William composed a new hymn that he set to a tune called, "The Officer's March" by Caroline Sheridan Norton. It became very popular and was published in the Millennial Star newspaper in 1863.

On June 3, 1863, William and Ellen answered the call and emigrated to America. It was a hard journey. "William's health was broken by the trials and physical stress of traveling across the plains. He contracted tuberculosis, which caused his premature death at the age of 35. He died just two years after emigrating to America." A monument was raised in his honor in Manti, where he taught school for a short time.

He may have had a short life, but oh, what a legacy. For you see, the new hymn written by this faithful, obedient pioneer was "We Thank Thee O God For A Prophet."

Maybe today there are some who don't sing it like they mean it, but it was written by a man whose life and sacrifice proved it.

Source:

J. Spencer Cornwall, Stories of our Mormon Hymns, Deseret Book, 1963, p. 207-11

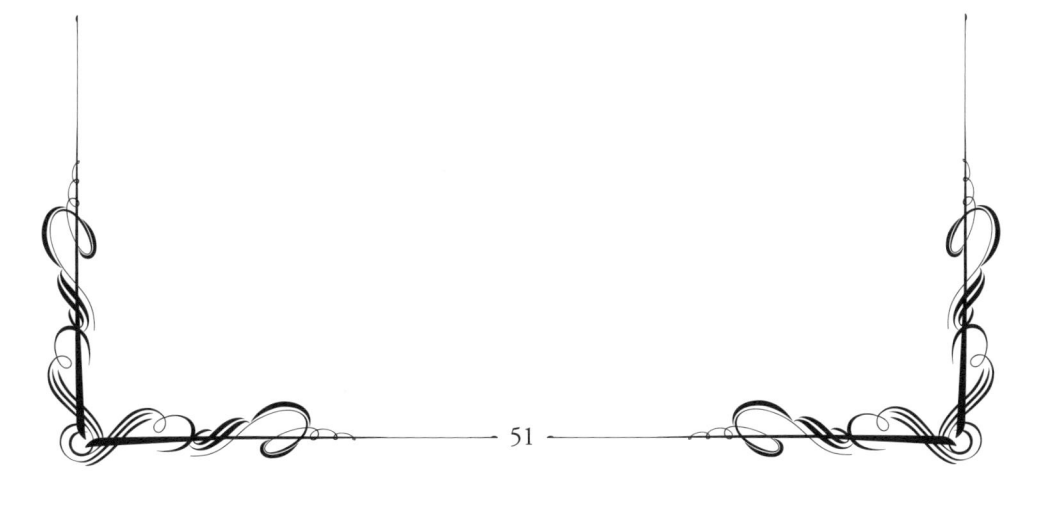

Zina Young Card

CHAPTER FOURTEEN

I Have Never Mourned One Moment Since

You may recall this event. It was Sunday afternoon, September 16, 1877 in the new Tabernacle in Salt Lake City, Utah when President Wilford Woodruff said the following near the close of his address:

> *I will here say, before closing, that two weeks before I left St. George, the spirits of the dead gathered around me, wanting to know why we did not redeem them. Said they, "You have had the use of the Endowment House for a number of years, and yet nothing has ever been done for us. We laid the foundation of the government you now enjoy, and we never apostatized from it, but we remained true to it and were faithful to God."*
>
> *These were the signers of the Declaration of Independence, and they waited on me for two days and two nights. I thought it very singular, that notwithstanding so much work had been done, and yet nothing had been done for them.... I straightway went into the baptismal font and called upon Brother McCallister to baptize me for the signers of the Declaration of Independence, and fifty other eminent men, making one hundred in all, including John Wesley, Columbus, and others; I then baptized him for every President of the United States, except three; and when their cause is just, somebody will do the work for them.*

As is often the case, there is a sequel to this fascinating story. It was May 1884, just after the dedication of the Logan Temple. Zina Young Card, daughter of Brigham Young, was riding the train from Logan to Salt Lake. President Woodruff was also on the train. He invited her to sit beside him. They began talking about the new temple. Then the conversation turned to President Woodruff's experiences in St. George. Zina records the following:

> *"Yes, yes," he said. "I received the great manifestations of my life while there. You and your mother know something of my plans for my 'Briggie' boy when he was drowned. (He is speaking of Brigham Young Woodruff, who passed away at the age of 20, in June 1877, and is buried in Smithfield, Utah.) He was to be my secretary and an assistant in the Historian's Office, and I did need him, too.*
>
> *He graduated in the best of trim for this work. Well, the trial seemed too hard to bear. As I was in St. George, I could not go home to comfort anybody, so I just went to the mountains up among the Indians where I fasted and prayed for strength to bear my sorrow, and to plead with the Lord to know why this had been sent to me.*
>
> *As I sat with my hands covering my face, I felt a spirit of peace, and looking up I saw Brother Brigham in a cloud of light standing some distance from the ground. O how beautiful and noble he looked. I sprang to my feet and I stretched out my arms to him, saying, 'Brother Brigham, you have come for me.'*
>
> *He smiled and answered, 'No, you have a great mission yet to perform on the earth. I came in answer to your prayers and to comfort you. Your Brigham had another mission to perform of greater importance. Do you recall the great work you have done and had done for your kindred dead, and the great men of the earth who have been done for in the Temple of the Lord? He is preaching to them and is the one to carry this great message of salvation to those who have and will receive the gospel in the Spirit World.'*

How glorious this message was to me....I asked, 'What should I tell the Saints?' He spoke with power, 'Tell them to wake up and live the gospel in their daily lives. We are so busy here working for you.' He smiled and seemed to enter into the cloud of light."

"Oh, how I humbled myself to the very earth, and praised God that I had a son worthy to do such a glorious work. Sister, I have never mourned one moment since for my boy."

Many years later, in 1928, Zina Young Card, now an elderly woman. would recount that experience in a letter to grieving family and friends. I share it now, similarly, to those who may be hurting and needing to know.

Source:

Family Records of Charles Ora and Zina Young Card. Copy of letter in Author's possession.

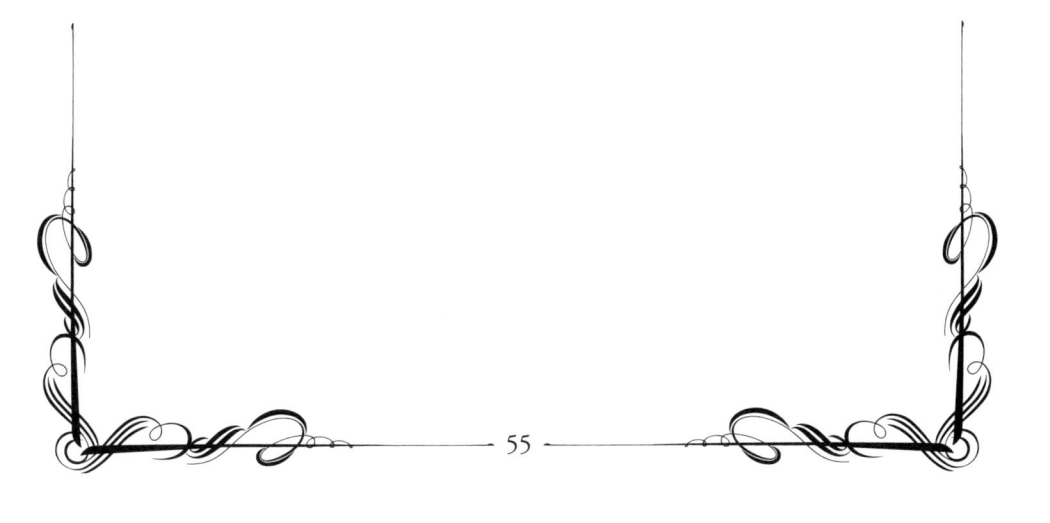

Brigham Young

CHAPTER FIFTEEN

The Mission of Mercy

Winter 1859, Cache Valley Utah. Brigham Young had called a small group of settlers under the direction of Peter Maughn to make permanent settlement in the then cold and forbidding Cache Valley of northern Utah. Upon arrival, the small group made huts and shelters against the coming winter, but the severity of the weather soon overpowered them. Many of them became ill. Food was running low and medical supplies were scarce.

Volunteers were requested to go over the mountains into Ogden and get the needed supplies. Three men volunteered- Thomas Lorenzo Obray, his brother Samuel, and George Hill. With ox-drawn wagons, they crossed over the mountains and reached Ogden with little difficulty. They obtained the precious food and supplies and prepared to start back. However, heavy snow had fallen in the mountains, making the journey, which normally took three days, much longer and more difficult.

Once in the high country, the men were forced to move ahead of the oxen shoveling a path through the snow. Then, one of their oxen took sick and fell to the ground. The men understood that they were now in a dangerous situation. They had to get off that mountain before they froze to death, but they couldn't make it without their oxen. They were desperate and afraid. It was then that Thomas suggested that, as men of the Priesthood, perhaps they should administer to the ailing animal.

"We are on a mission of mercy for our people," he said. "We have answered the call of those who are in authority, and we all know that by the laying on of hands and asking for the help of the Lord, he can heal us. With so many lives at stake and depending upon us, He surely can heal the ox."

The men knelt and prayed, asking the Almighty to bless the beast. They then administered to him just as they would have a man. They covered him with a blanket and let the ox rest. A few hours later, they returned and pulled the blanket off. The ox stood up and shook his body as if to restore circulation. They yoked him up and went on their way, arriving successfully in the snowbound valley with the precious load of food and medicine.

I understand the properties of the priesthood. But, sometimes I wonder if we tend to put God and his prophets in a box limiting what they can say and do for our blessing and benefit. Our God is mighty to save. He has all power and all knowledge.

Source:

https://www.familysearch.org/tree/person/memories/KWZY-XD8

Story Contributed by Harold Obray

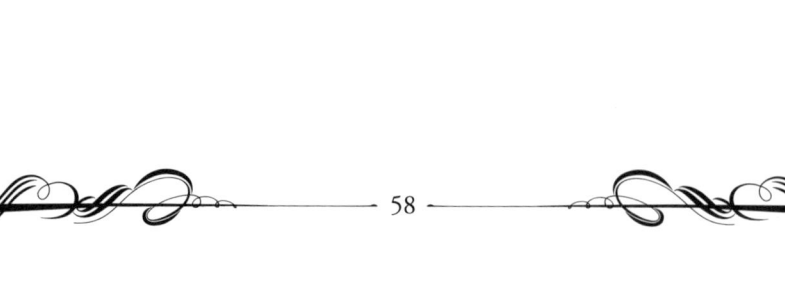

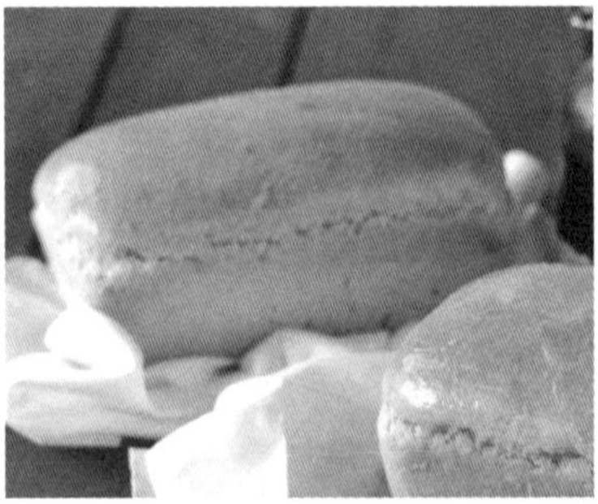

CHAPTER SIXTEEN

The Miracle Loaf of Bread

James Fisher left a wife and three children to answer a call to serve as a missionary in New Zealand. For three years and four months, he served faithfully while his wife ran the farm, raised the children, and worked diligently to support him.

One day, while Elder Fisher and his companion were riding along on their horses, they started talking about home as missionaries will often do. "They talked about how much they missed the good, homemade bread so common back in Utah. Money from home had not yet arrived and they were, quite simply, hungry.

Elder Fisher's companion suggested that they were alone and could dismount. They went into the woods and prayed. They expressed their desire to serve, as well as their love and concern for those back home. The two elders felt better, got back on their horses, and continued on their way. As they rode along, they noticed something just off the road.

They dismounted and to their amazement found, wrapped in a white cloth, a fresh loaf of bread, the same kind of homemade bread they had talked about in their prayer. They rejoiced as they ate it, although it wasn't the bread that was so important, but the reassurance that Heavenly Father knew who they were and where they were, that they had faithful wives and that the Lord's kindness and goodness was over them all."

Of course, both missionaries wrote home and told their wives of the miracle. Postage was expensive and mail traveled slowly. About three months after the event, Elder Fisher's companion received a letter from his wife. She told him that on the day they received their miracle loaf of bread "she had been baking bread, and when she opened the oven to take it out, one of the pans was empty and a white cloth that had been on the table was gone."

Two humble missionaries received a tender mercy from the Lord. "The loaf of bread came to symbolize for them that it was Heavenly Father who had sent them to New Zealand and that he was supporting and watching over their families. Incidentally, when James returned home, the farm had prospered and he and his wife owned more cattle and sheep and had more money than before . . . . Because of their willingness to sacrifice in the service of the Lord, they received miraculous blessings."

Source:

https://www.familysearch.org/tree/person/memories/KWCX-DCX

Story contributed by Dorcas Anderson of Burley Idaho. James Fisher was her great grandfather.

Elder Ted E. Brewerton, New Era, November 1990

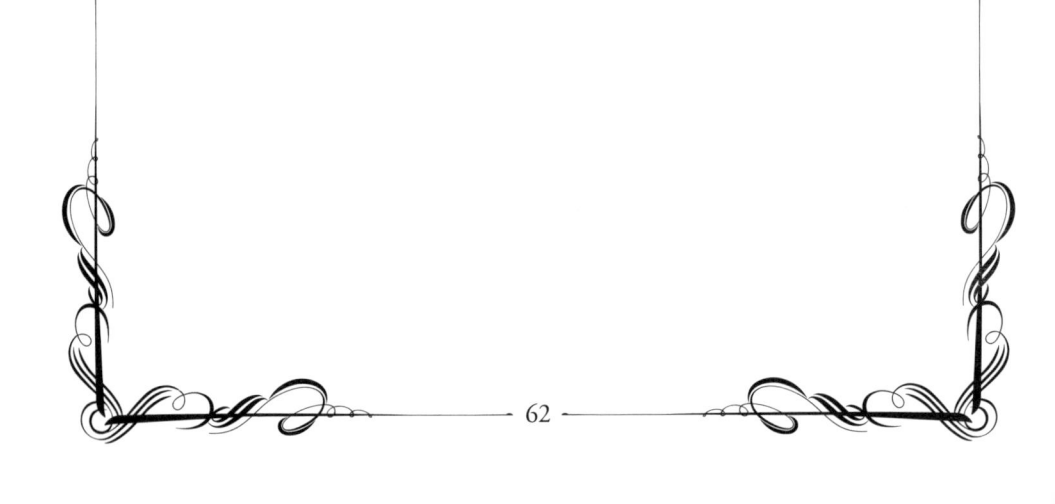

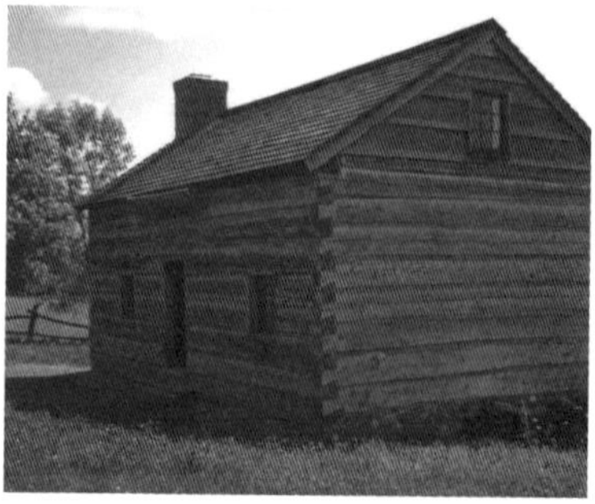

CHAPTER SEVENTEEN

Ezra Thayer and The Book of Mormon

One morning in the fall of 1825, an old gentleman went on his way through the New York countryside singing joyfully. As he approached the door of a farmhouse, the owner, Ezra Thayer, opened the door. "Good morning, sir," said the old stranger. Ezra returned the greeting. "Do you ever give a stranger and a poor traveler something to eat?" he said, and Ezra replied, "always."

Ezra described that he had never heard the hymn the old man was singing, but it seemed to "lighten up my soul,' he said, "and filled it with the Spirit of the Lord." While his wife prepared the breakfast, the old man asked Ezra questions which Ezra could not answer. The old man would smile and continue singing.

Ezra said, "After eating [he] put his chair back and continued with his singing for a little. Then he arose and left the choicest blessings for me and my house and bid me goodbye. He stepped on the doorstep and as he let down the latch, I lifted it. As I opened the door, there was no man there. He could not possibly have gone out of my way, for I could see 40 or 50 rods all around. I searche[d] every place for him. I called my wife out and we were astonished above all measure. I made mention of it 8 or 10 miles from home and they said there had been just such a man who had been heard of in different places."

As time passed, other unusual and extraordinary manifestations were given to Ezra. Then, in the fall of 1830, he began hearing rumors about Joseph Smith and a new book he had translated called the Book of Mormon. Thayer considered the story blasphemous and "was filled with wrath about it."

Ezra Thayer had known the Smith family. They had worked for him, and the idea that the uneducated Joseph Smith Jr. had the capacity to translate and publish a book of scripture was preposterous and impossible.

When some of his family showed an interest in learning more about the Book of Mormon, Thayer was angry. When some family members took his horses and went to hear Hyrum Smith preach, Thayer scolded them and demanded that they "not take [his] horses again to hear those blasphemous wretches preach." In fact, he was angry enough that he offered to loan "a pair of horses [to take Joseph Smith] to prison."

Though his family insisted there was something to the message and that he ought to give it a chance, he remained aloof and angry. Finally, his brother came and asked him to go and hear the preaching. After all, what harm could come in just listening. Reluctantly, Ezra agreed to go.

It was Sunday, October 5, 1830 when the two brothers rode up to the Smith Family log cabin in Palmyra Township. There was a large spreading crowd gathered around to hear Hyrum preach. Ezra "rushed in and got close to the stand, so as to be particular to hear what was said." He said, "When Hyrum began to preach, every word touched me to the inmost soul. I thought every word was pointed to me. . . . I could not help myself. The tears rolled down my cheeks, I was very proud and stubborn. There were many there who knew me. . . . When Hyrum got through, he picked up a book and said, 'Here is the Book of Mormon.' I said, 'Let me see it.' I then opened the book, and I received a shock with such exquisite joy that no pen can write and no tongue can express. I shut the book and said, "What is the price of it?"

"Fourteen shillings," was the reply. I said, "I'll take the book." I opened it again, and I felt a double portion of the Spirit, and I did not know whether I was in the world or not. I felt as though I was truly in heaven.

As Ezra and his brother started for home, his brother asked what he thought of the Book of Mormon, Ezra answered "It is true as sure as God sits upon his throne."

Soon thereafter, Ezra Thayer was baptized and called on a mission. At his request, the Lord gave a revelation to Ezra Thayer. Three times he was commanded to open his mouth and the Almighty would fill it. Ezra was faithful and immediately set out preaching the gospel. As he declared it, "When God shows a man such a thing by the power of the Holy Ghost, he knows it is true. He cannot doubt it." And of the Book of Mormon, Ezra never did. There is a power in the Book of Mormon that is off the grid for mortals to comprehend.

Source:

http://www.sidneyrigdon.com/dbroadhu/OH/sain1860.htm

https://www.churchofjesuschrist.org/study/manual/revelations-in-context/ezra-thayer-from-skeptic-to-believer?lang=eng

https://www.josephsmithpapers.org/person/ezra-thayer

John and Alice

CHAPTER EIGHTEEN

Such A Great Sacrifice

John Alexander Clark was a beloved son of Ezra and Susan Legget Clark. He was a bright, well-educated, adventurous young man who loved life and learning. In 1893, he was teaching school in Minersville, Utah.

His sister, Alice, to whom he was particularly close wrote this of the sudden change in their relationship, "Into every life comes sunshine and shadows and a cloud now darkened my sky. John received a letter, which ended our close association. It was a call to the Turkish Mission…. His leaving caused indescribable loneliness and gloom for me, but when he asked me if I was sorry he was going, I replied with all the cheerfulness possible, 'No. I'll try not to be, as it is the Father's calling."

John was given three months to prepare. He left in February 1894. He journeyed to Liverpool, England and then on to his field of labor. He loved the people and had an aptitude for the German and Arabic languages the people spoke. His love for the people drove him to reach out to all. Because of that, he came in contact with Black Smallpox and on January 30, 1895, became ill. He passed away just after midnight February 8, 1895. He was hastily buried in an unmarked grave and his belongings destroyed.

His family was devastated by the news. His mother, Susan, wrote to the family with whom John had lived. She said, "Will you please write, and tell one all the particulars of his sickness and death and burial and what his last words were.... Oh, Sister Hilt, I cannot see why the Lord did not spare his life, or send an angel to heal him. He was so good, so noble, or do you think his task was done here, and he was needed on the other side? Did he not express a desire to live? Tell me all you can concerning him."

His beloved sister, Alice, was a student at BYU when she learned of John's death. She mourned for weeks and nearly failed school. "One day, I returned from school in a despondent and listless mood," she said. "The following morning, I experienced a very unusual manifestation. John's voice, as plainly as when he was alive, quoted the same words he had spoken just before he left. "You said you were not sorry I was going on a mission, now why are you? She replied, 'I'll try not to be anymore.'"

Another sister, Annie, described her feelings. "It is poor comfort to be told that they have gone to a better world. We need the bright, intelligent ones here. We want their companionship. When out in the backyard with my little children, I pulled my sunbonnet down to hide my face, wet with tears, and it seemed that John would try to comfort me. 'We must be reconciled to His will,' I imagined him saying, and then I wondered why His will required such a great sacrifice. Of course, John's body could not be brought home."

The local Farmington newspaper wrote of John, "The deceased was an excellent young man worthy of the high confidence placed in him, and the news of his death, while he was yet on the threshold of manhood, will be received with universal sadness and regret."

The family could not bring his body home and as far as the record shows, his parents were never able to visit his final resting place. They sent money to have a monument erected in his honor. It was such a tragedy. Such a loss—and some may say, 'all for no purpose!' But was it?

John was a teacher. He loved books, learning, and people. Little could his family know in 1895 that his tragic death would one day help open the way for priceless educational opportunities for thousands of eager young people. For you see, John was serving as a missionary in what would one day become the modern state of Israel. Decades later, when The Church of Jesus Christ of Latter-day Saints needed proof that they had an official presence in the country previous to 1948, the grave of John Alexander Clark, lying at the foot of Mt. Carmel near Haifa, helped establish that presence and the Jerusalem Center was built.

Source:

From various articles and documents at:

https://www.familysearch.org/tree/person/memories/KWVC-CXC

Art (On Left)

CHAPTER NINETEEN

I Have Been Praying For You To Come

The year was 1961. Art Johansen had just received a call to serve for 2 ½ years in the French East Mission. Shortly after, he was at a ward activity where he told his former Priest Quorum Advisor, Marvyn Hogenson, about his call. To his surprise, Marvyn told the young elder he was sorry he was being called to that mission. He had served in that same mission 12 years earlier. He said it was an extremely difficult area to serve in and felt his mission was a failure. He doubted that he had made a difference in anyone's life.

Elder Johansen went to France. In time, he was assigned to labor in the city of Marseille. He and his senior companion tracted 70 hours a week for three weeks with no success. One day, his companion, understandably a little discouraged, suggested they take a break and go buy a pastry. However, Elder Johansen had a strong feeling they needed to continue tracting through the next building. His companion reluctantly agreed.

They went to the next building. It was a four-story building with four apartments on each level. The missionaries went to the top level and knocked on all four doors–no answer. The same thing happened on the third floor. On the second floor, on the third door they knocked, a Swiss-German lady answered. She said, "Elders. I have been praying for you to come. I want to be baptized. Come in."

She pulled out a well-worn copy of the Book of Mormon and a Joseph Smith pamphlet she had been given years before by another missionary. He spoke only French and she spoke only German. Hence, their contact had ended with the book.

Over the years, she had studied the Book of Mormon often and she knew it well. She even called together family and friends and they studied the book together. She was ready.

Elder Johansen and his companion taught her all of the missionary lessons and she and her nine-year-old daughter were baptized 10 days later. The Elders then began to teach her other children and the people she referred to them. Before it was through, more than 50 people had joined the Church, and that because of a simple exchange between two people with limited communication.

There is one more part to this story. When Elder Johansen looked at the hand-written name scrawled on the pamphlet, can you imagine his reaction when he saw the name "Elder Marvyn Hoganson?" It was his former Priest Quorum Advisor—the one who thought his mission had made no difference in anyone's life.

You see, the Lord's hand is in the details. Some will sow and some will reap, and the Book of Mormon is the great power of the Lord's harvest.

Source:

Art Johansen and family of Utah

Marvyn William Hogenson Family Search # LFFM-DG4

Ingrid Larson Pehrson

CHAPTER TWENTY

The Power of Sacred Music

The lyrics and melody of hymns open the way for the Spirit to touch the hearts of God's children. This is a story of a faithful member missionary who shared her testimony through music.

Ingrid Larson Pehrson lived in Vingaker, Sweden on a rented farm with her five young children, Anna, Hulda, Carolina, Gustave, and Marie. Life was not easy, especially since her husband, Pehr Gustave Pehrson, had passed away from pneumonia the previous year, two weeks after she gave birth to her youngest child. With the help of a hired man, she worked in the fields and cared for her growing family.

One day, a single woman named Brita Maria Larson, who earned her living by spinning and weaving for others, came to Ingrid's home to spin. While she worked, she sang hymns. Ingrid and her children loved hearing the songs. They were especially captivated by the lyrics of the hymn *O My Father*. The words of the hymn seemed to speak to the hearts of the grieving family.

They asked Brita where she had learned the songs, and she told them she was a member of the Mormon Church (The Church of Jesus Christ of Latter-day Saints). Ingrid had heard the negative rumors about this religion circulated in the community, but she saw this woman was someone special and nothing like the bad things she'd heard.

Brita came again and this time brought a Book of Mormon and other literature for the family to read. Ingrid diligently studied and attended meetings with the missionaries in people's homes. Against the wishes of her father, she joined the Church in 1889 and over the next few years, her children were also baptized. Within 10 years, the entire family immigrated to Utah.

As a humble member missionary, Brita was happy for the part she played in introducing six people to the gospel. What the musically inclined saint didn't know was that her simple act of sharing the hymns of the restoration would open the door for a posterity of over 1,500 people to enjoy the blessings of the Gospel of Jesus Christ across the generations.

Source:

Story contributed by Jean Tonioli

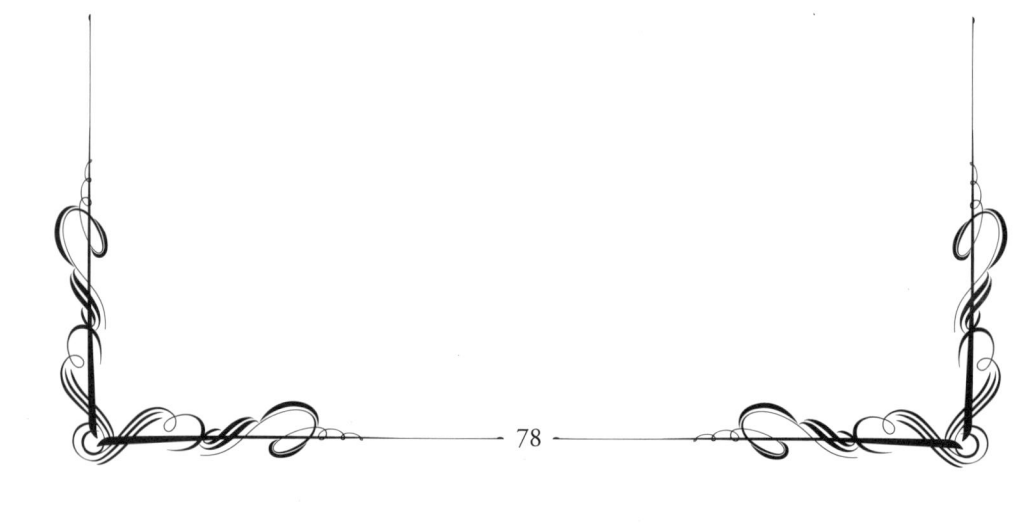

Horatio Spafford

CHAPTER TWENTY-ONE

It Is Well With My Soul

Horatio Spafford came to Chicago in 1856 to practice law. He was a devoutly religious man and soon formed associations with other evangelical Christians, Reverend Moody and others. In those early days in Chicago, Spafford wasn't just a "Sunday go to meeting" kind of Christian. He put his Christianity into practice, notwithstanding he was a lawyer, he taught Sunday School classes, visited the sick and imprisoned, and ministered where he could.

In 1857, he first met Anna Larsson. She was a somewhat recent convert from Norway. Horatio was taken with her beauty, poise and self-confidence. However, she was only 15-years-old. Spafford paid for Anna to attend an elite women's school. After graduation three years later, at the age of 18, they were married.

During the Civil War, Horatio and Anna volunteered and served the cause wherever they could. Horatio continued as a lawyer, senior partner in their firm, and as a professor of law. In 1870, the "odyssey of Job" began. Their four-year-old son, Horatio Jr. died of scarlet fever. Then, a year later in October 1871, the great Chicago fire broke out and reduced Chicago to ashes taking with it most of Horatio's considerable real estate investments. Notwithstanding their loss, the Spaffords worked to assist others stricken by the fire.

In 1873, the family decided to take a holiday to Europe. At the last minute, Horatio was detained because of business in the city and sent his wife and four remaining children on ahead. It was Anna and her 11-year-old daughter, also named Anna, nine-year-old Margaret, five-year-old Elizabeth, and two-year-old Tanetta.

On November 22, 1873, their ship, the Ville Du Havre, was rammed midships by an iron vessel, the Lochearn. The Ville Du Havre sank in 12 minutes. It would be one of the worst maritime disasters in the 19th century, until the sinking of the Titanic. 226 people lost their lives. Among them were the four daughters of Horatio and Anna Spafford. At the collision, Ann gathered her children close, looked for escape, and attempted to comfort and assist other passengers, but as the ship tipped onto its bow and started under, the babe Tanetta was torn from her arms and swept away, as were the other girls. In the end, the four girls either drowned or succumbed to the icy waters of the North Atlantic.

Anna, by some miracle, was found floating semi-conscious on a piece of planking. After her rescue, she was overheard to say, "God gave me four daughters. Now they have been taken from me. Someday I will understand why." She would later testify that in anguish and grief, she heard a still small voice speaking to her, "You were saved for a purpose."

When she arrived in Cardiff, South Wales, she sent a telegram to her husband that read simply, "Saved alone. What shall I do?"

Horatio immediately boarded another ship and set out to join Anna in Wales. As they sailed, it is reported that one day, the captain called Spafford to the bridge, pointed to his navigation charts, and informed him they were passing over the very spot where the Ville du Havre went down.

Spafford returned to his cabin and, with emotions we can only imagine, wrote these words, "When peace like a river attendeth my way, when sorrow like sea billows roll; Whatever my lot,

Thou hast taught me to know It is well, it is well, with my soul...." It would become the beloved Christian hymn "It Is Well With My Soul."

A few days later, his faith shone through again as he wrote in a letter to his sister-in-law, "On Thursday last, we passed over the spot where she went down, in mid-ocean, the waters three miles deep. But I do not think of our dear ones there. They are safe.... dear lambs."

The Spaffords returned to Chicago where three more children were born to them, but, like Job, was it the end of their loss and sorrow? No! Their only son, born after they returned to Chicago, died at the age of four. It is said that people of their congregation began to talk ill, "What had the Spaffords done to so offend God and bring upon themselves so much misfortune?" I can't imagine such cruel talk.

The Spaffords made a decision. Horatio and Anna Spafford left Chicago, and their church, and became independent, free-thinking Christians. They emigrated to Jerusalem, where they established the famous American Colony. There Horatio and Anna lived out their days practicing the full measure of Christianity as they understood it. All were loved and served, and all were welcomed and ministered to. They gave all they had in a land of enemies and allies. They took no sides. Today, Horatio and Anna Spafford are both buried in Jerusalem, awaiting that day they so longed for when the Lord would return and call them up. Indeed, it is well with their souls. Is it well with yours?

Source:

https://www.bethelripon.com/life-stories/horatio-gates-spafford

https://www.loc.gov/exhibits/americancolony/amcolony-family.html

https://en.wikipedia.org/wiki/It_Is_Well_with_My_Soul

https://www.loc.gov/exhibits/americancolony/amcolony-family.html

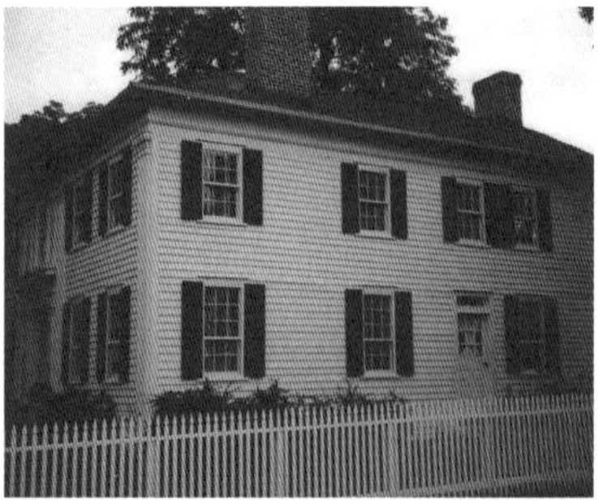

CHAPTER TWENTY-TWO

Brother Joseph Gave Me His Hand

John Harper was born on March 9, 1813, in County Down, Ireland, the son of James and Sarah Blair Harper. He was baptized June 6, 1841, in Glasgow, Scotland. On December 31, 1842, John and his wife Margaret sailed from Scotland to Liverpool and on to Nauvoo. Their voyage was a difficult crossing, but finally, on April 12, 1842, John and Margaret landed at Nauvoo. John records that moment stepping off the boat in Nauvoo. You can see it. You can picture this. He said:

> "We were met at the landing by the Prophet of the Lord and some of the twelve apostles and a great number of the Saints. I was then fully rewarded for all that I had passed, to see with my eyes and hear with my ears a living Prophet of [the] God of Israel."

What a sweet testimony. John eventually found work on the Nauvoo House and then on the Nauvoo Temple. It was while engaged in that labor that John tells the following story.

> "In the month of December [1843], I became very bad with a violent pain in my right side. It was excruciating. I had been bad from the 26th to the evening of the 27th, when through solicitation of my dear wife and the help of a cane, we went out to get some of the Twelve to administer to me. I came to the Mansion House, where the Prophet lived. I went into the bar room and asked Brother Lorin Walker if Brother Joseph was in and he said 'yes,' and he went upstairs and told him

to come down. I told him that I was very sick with a pain in my side. He said, 'Sit down.' He laid his hands on my head and rebuked the pain in the name of the Lord. When he took his hands off my head, I was healed and went home rejoicing in the God of my salvation and have never been troubled with it since that time."

There's more. John and Margaret were there when Joseph and Hyrum were killed at Carthage. They were there in Nauvoo in August of 1844 to witness the transformation of Brigham Young and they were there as time went on and the mobs began to threaten the saints. It was during those difficulties that John relates the following. (I've never read this. I've never seen it in print anywhere. I found it on Family Search in the records of John Harper. I know I'm not the scholar who knows everything, but I've never seen this in print, and I loved it.) I quote John. I found it in his autobiography where he said:

"I became desirous to be ordained [to the priesthood] (now this is during the mob actions going on in Nauvoo) and in the month of August I had a very pleasant dream.

Listen to this. This is so pregnant with symbolism. He said:

"I thought I was going up a very high mountain and I had got within about two or three steps of the top [and] tried to ascend but could not get up. I tried again, but it seemed impossible. Then Brother Joseph gave me his hand and took me up to the top [and] told me to sit down. He laid his hands on my head and ordained me an Elder in The Church of Jesus Christ of Latter-Day Saints."

Not too long after that wonderful dream, on August 19, 1844, John saw the fulfillment of his dream. He was ordained to the office of an Elder in the Melchizedek priesthood. "Truly," he said, "my heart was made to rejoice in thanks to God and my Heavenly Father that I had been permitted to hold the Holy Priesthood."

Imagine cherishing the priesthood that much. Now, my dear friends, I speak with testimony and earnestness. There is much we can do. In fact, most of the world seeks to draw near to God no matter what name they may call Him. Our God is a merciful god and He has a measure of salvation for all the human family that will. But exaltation is another matter.

Joseph Smith the Prophet holds the Savior's presiding priesthood authority and keys over this last dispensation. He still presides and directs this work as the authorized Priesthood President in the world of spirits. All men who would ascend unto the fullness of Christ and the highest of exaltation must and will come unto that authority.

Source:

https://www.familysearch.org/tree/person/memories/KWJD-V3F

Glenn and His Girls

CHAPTER TWENTY-THREE

Daddy, Help!

Please consider this verse: "[The devil] is the founder of murder, and works of darkness; yea, and he leadeth them by the neck with a flaxen cord, until he bindeth them with his strong cords forever." (2 Nephi 26:22). From a tender, flaxen cord to an unbreakable, strong bond, the devil's intent is to destroy our agency and thereby destroy us. My family recently learned a terrifying lesson.

My beautiful daughters, Sherise, Dawni Jo, and Annie wanted to climb the South Peak of the Three Tetons in Wyoming. In preparation, we called ahead, talked to the Rangers, and got ready.

On the day of the hike, we left in good time and started up the mountain. Other than a little altitude queasiness, we did okay. On the way up, we encountered snow fields that we were not expecting. I'd been up on that mountain several times before and had never seen this much snow that late in the season. We managed to skirt most of them and kept going. We came to one snowfield, however, just below the lower saddle. It was long, wide, and steep. We could not go around it.

There was a good trail with deep footholds going across, so we decided to proceed. We made it to the Lower Saddle, and all was well. It was a glorious view and we did the Instagram thing. We decided not to try and make it to the summit of the

South Teton. Weather was threatening and it was getting late. We started back down and came to that same long snowfield.

The alternate route I had planned around it turned out to be untenable. We had to come down the way we went up, but now the snow was softer and the trail more dangerous. We did not have the proper equipment. We were told we didn't need it, but now we needed it and we had no choice but to go on. I started out ahead cutting footholds, my daughters coming behind me. I was praying continually when suddenly the thought came to me, "sit down and slide."

I looked down the slope. It was probably more than 300 feet down and probably more than 45% slope with boulders at the bottom. In short, it was dumb and dangerous. I hesitated a moment and the thought came again. So, I sat down and let go. I picked up speed so fast that for a moment I wondered what I had done. Desperately, I dug my hands and heels into the snow as far as I could, throwing snow like a plow, but still I picked up speed. It felt as though every bit of skin on my hands was being shredded. I was on a course of imminent injury. Then, just before the boulders, the snow softened even more, and I plunged my hands and heels deeper. Somehow it slowed me without flipping me over. I still hit the bottom hard enough to kiss the rocks, but not seriously.

I stood for a moment trying to shake the pain out of my hands, when I suddenly heard a cry, "Daddy, Help!" I looked up in time to see my oldest daughter Sherise completely out of control and barreling down the slope. I took off running to intercept, but I wasn't going to make it. She plowed through some rocks sticking up in the snow and then a split second later hit dry ground, folding up like a pocketknife and going head-first into the boulders. For a moment she did not move, and then slowly began to come to. There was no way to know how badly she was injured, but it was clear she was hurt. After a few minutes, she asked me for a blessing. Right there on the mountain, I blessed her to be well and attended by angels. A few minutes later she stood up, and, moving slowly, made her way off the mountain. She was bruised more deeply than I have ever seen, but by some miracle nothing was broken and there was no permanent damage.

She later told me what happened. She was the last in the procession on the snowfield. She watched me slide down and knew she was not going to try that. She stepped forward with her right foot and as her weight came down on it, it slid out from under her—slowly at first. She thought, "I got this," but when she tried to pull it back, the left foot gave way. In a moment, she was completely out of control and all she could think of was to scream, "daddy, help!" I still hear her voice in my head. I don't think I will ever forget it.

How much like life is Sherise's experience. Some of us in this life venture into places we should not go. We think we can handle it. We step out onto slippery slopes and before we even know what is happening, we are sliding out of control.

It would be trite and cruel to say we should never step into such dangerous territory, but we do—we all do! I can't tell you how many times I've found myself where I shouldn't be and injury always followed. But somehow, somewhere I learned that in such moments I should cry, "Daddy, Help!" I have, and my Heavenly Father has always met me at the bottom, blessed me, and got me back on my feet.

Source:

Rawson Family Experience July 2020 Teton Range Wyoming.

Emma Smith

CHAPTER TWENTY-FOUR

A Cohort of Angels

In the early decades of the nineteenth century, American's did not celebrate Christmas according to the customs of our day. It was, however, a day to gather with family and friends. For the Prophet Joseph Smith, not every Christmas had been pleasant. In 1837, persecution mounted in Kirtland and within days, over Christmas, Joseph had to flee for his life to Missouri. In 1838, Joseph and several of his friends had spent Christmas in the Liberty Jail. In 1839, he spent the holiday season in Washington, D.C., being spurned by politicians as he went there seeking compensation for church members who had lost their belongings to mobs in Missouri. Christmas of 1842, he met with Governor Ford about difficulties between Saints and their nonmember neighbors in Illinois.

Sometimes in this life, we are blessed with one of those perfect days that remains in our memories forever. Such was the kind of day Joseph Smith had on December 25, 1843 – his last Christmas on earth. He had just moved his family into the newly constructed Mansion House. All was quiet and at peace in Nauvoo. Then around 1:00 a.m. on Christmas morning, Joseph and Emma were awakened in the Mansion House by singing outside their bedroom window. Joseph recorded this in his journal:

"Christmas 1843: Monday, 25.- This morning, about one o'clock, I was aroused by an English sister, Lettice Rushton,

widow of Richard Rushton, Senior, (who, ten years ago, lost her sight,) accompanied by three of her sons, with their wives, and her two daughters, with their husbands, and several of her neighbors, singing, 'Mortals, awake! with angels join,' which caused a thrill of pleasure to run through my soul. All of my family and boarders arose to hear the serenade, and I felt to thank my Heavenly Father for their visit and blessed them in the name of the Lord. They also visited my brother Hyrum, who was awakened from his sleep. He arose and went out of doors. He shook hands with and blessed each one of them in the name of the Lord and said that he thought at first that a cohort of angels had come to visit him, it was such heavenly music to him."

Later that day Joseph and Emma Smith invited fifty couples to their home for a mid afternoon meal. During the evening, many people stopped by for food, music, and even dancing. Christmas Day 1843 was a day which began with songs praising the Lord and continued in the company of family and friends who valued him the most.

It would be Joseph Smith's last Christmas in mortality. Six months later, the Lord Jesus Christ whose special witness he was, called the prophet home.

Source:

Thanks to Jean Tonioli for her research on this story.

https://www.familysearch.org/tree/person/memories/LZRW-8WW

https://www.familysearch.org/tree/person/memories/KWJY-FP3

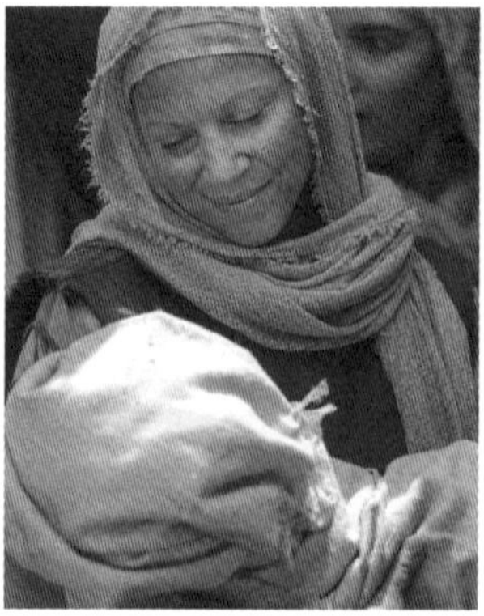

Chapter Twenty-Five

Christmas and John the Baptist

Have you ever noticed how often we tell the story of Christmas and skip over the birth of John the Baptist? I don't think we should. To neglect John in telling that story is like neglecting your preparations for Christmas until the morning of. Before there was John the Baptist, there was John the baby. Before Matthew, Mark, Luke, and John wrote of Jesus, John the Baptist kept a record first. As in his life, John pointed people to Jesus, and so too did he in his birth.

Before Gabriel came to Mary, he appeared to an old man named Zacharias in the Temple.

"Fear not, Zacharias," he said, "thy prayer is heard; and thy wife Elizabeth shall bear thee a son, and thou shalt call his name John."

The angel promised that this little boy would bring much joy to many people, but not just because he was a baby, but because he would "be great in the sight of the Lord…. Many of the children of Israel shall he turn to the Lord their God," Gabriel prophesied.

John would go before the Savior and "make ready a people prepared for the Lord."

Zacharias struggled to believe what he was hearing. I don't blame him. Elizabeth was an old woman, past the age of childbearing. Nonetheless, Mary's miraculous conception was not the first. Before Mary went into hiding with a child she couldn't explain, Elizabeth was there first.

One day a beautiful young woman sent by an angel comes into the courtyard of Elizabeth's home, and calls out a greeting. In the womb, John leaps for joy, and he and his mother are filled with the Holy Ghost. It is sublime that at that powerful moment, John bears witness of the Messiah before he even has a voice. The two sons of prophecy and their sainted mothers spend the next three months together. As John prepared the way for Jesus, so Elizabeth prepared and consoled Mary.

Before the people heard the shepherd's witness of a coming Messiah, they were astonished at the new voice and testimony of Zacharias. His prophecies resonated through the Judean hills and hearts of the Jews, filling them with grand expectations. Then and later, all who ever knew John couldn't wait to meet Jesus.

On the night of the Savior's birth in Bethlehem, John was three months old in Hebron. Knowing what Elizabeth knew of Mary and the bond they shared, I wonder how far away she really was from her young cousin.

When Herod's soldiers came, you know they were looking for two famous babies—not one. While the angel sent Joseph and Mary into Egypt to save Jesus, Zacharias sent John and Elizabeth into the wilderness. Joseph and Jesus escaped, but the soldiers killed Zacharias. He would not give up his son. As Jesus grew up with His father Joseph, hewing wood, so John grew up in the wilderness, without Zacharias, eating locusts and wild honey. As Jesus waited and prepared to bring men to His Father, so John waited and prepared to bring men to Jesus.

As Luke's story of Christmas tells of a special babe whose birth pointed men to Jesus' birth—as John was born to prepare the way—may we be reminded this Christmas that we too are born to prepare the way. The Messiah is coming—soon. You were born to bear witness of the Lord Jesus Christ and His restored gospel authority. God grant that we be like John, that in all that we are, all that we say, and all that we do, men want to meet Him.

C. H. Stoddard

CHAPTER TWENTY-SIX

Almost an Angel

Margaret Pierce Young was born in Aston Township, Delaware County, Pennsylvania. She said, "My parents, Robert and Hannah, were Quakers. My mother was well educated, a gifted writer and spiritually inclined. My father," she said, "was a prosperous farmer." Well, her parents lived in various parts of Pennsylvania but then in 1832, as fate would have it, they moved to Brandywine. She said, "Our house was beautifully situated on a low hill affording a fine view of a large part of our farm, which was green and pretty." It sat about 45 miles from Philadelphia.

She says, "When I was but a young girl, I took cold (meaning she got a cold) on the ice ponds and fever and heart trouble followed." She said, "I was ill for many months." Then she describes that, "One evening two men passing our way stopped and knocked at our door and announced, 'We are Latter-day Saints and have been directed to this house by the Spirit. Have you sickness here?' to which Margaret's mother answered, 'Yes, come in!'" She brought them to Margaret's bedside. The two men took Margaret by the hand, looked down on her for just a moment and then, turning to her mother, said, "If she will obey the Gospel of Christ and put her trust in Him, who is able to save, she will be healed from this very moment."

And then the two men, not identifying themselves, refused to sit down or take any refreshments. They left and went on their way. Margaret said, "I was healed and next morning was on my feet. We knew not who these servants of God were, from whence they came, nor did we ever after hear aught concerning them."

In the summer of 1839, shortly thereafter, there came two elders preaching the Gospel of Christ in that area. They were Elijah Davis and Lorenzo Barnes. Margaret said, "From them we heard the gospel explained in its fullness and in power. Their words sank deep into our hearts." The first baptisms resulted on the 29th of July and on 28th of October, following, the Brandywine Branch was organized. "Weekly meetings were held" Margaret said, "at our house, which was commodious and freely opened. People came from miles around to hear the principles of Mormonism expounded."

In January of 1840, word came, at the Brandywine branch, that Joseph Smith the prophet was going to pay them a visit on his way from Philadelphia. Margaret's father said, "Let us get our carriage and go to meet him. So," she said, "father, and others brought him to our home. Mother served a splendid supper and then the neighbors gathered in to hear the Prophet's discourse. I wish that I might describe my feelings at that meeting. Though they are fresh and green in my memory today, I cannot but fall short of expressing myself. So animated with loving kindness, so mild and gentle, yet big and powerful and majestic was the Prophet that to me he seemed more than a man. I thought almost an angel. We were all investigating but none of my people had entered the waters of baptism, however it was a great joy to us to entertain Joseph Smith and hear his wonderful words of wisdom." She continued, "It was 2 o'clock in the morning when we permitted him to retire. I wanted to listen to him all night." When the Prophet was finally allowed to go to bed and had left the room, Margaret said, "My mother said, 'I don't see how anyone can doubt his being a Prophet of God. [You] can see it in his countenance which is so full of intelligence.' 'Yes, truly,' Father replied, 'He is a Prophet of God.'"

The next day, Margaret's mother was ready for baptism. The ice was 6 inches thick. They cut it, and she entered the waters of baptism, receiving that ordinance under the hands of Elder Lorenzo Barnes and was confirmed by the Prophet Joseph. Margaret's sister Mary followed, but Mother made Margaret wait until the weather was milder. So, it was April 1840 when Margaret became a member of the Church. Her father joined the day after she did. Then her father sold all of his property with the fixed purpose of gathering with the Saints. "One lovely day 22 September 1841," she said, "we bade farewell to the land of our Quaker parentage. Traveling by rail and by steamboat, we soon landed in beautiful Nauvoo. At the landing, who should meet us but the Prophet and his wife, who took us home and entertained us most hospitably. Their family was always very friendly to all of us, seeming never to forget my Father's hospitality in Pennsylvania."

Source:

https://www.familysearch.org/tree/person/memories/LC7D-4V8

Sarah D. Rich

CHAPTER TWENTY - SEVEN

George, Do You Know Me?

April 12, 1847, Elm Grove, Iowa. Sarah De Armon Pea Rich recorded in her autobiography for this day, "While here the boy that was with us--George Patten was taken very sick with the Mountain Fever."

George Patten was just a boy. His mother had passed away in Nauvoo and his father had given him to Charles and Sarah Rich to take with them to the Rocky Mountains. Sarah continued, "And on the 22nd of April 1847, some of the company started on... and the boy that was with us--still very sick."

The company traveled on until they reached Garden Grove, Iowa, where they remained for a month. On May 22, 1847, Sarah wrote, "Our boy, George Patten, still got worse and became as helpless as a babe— was out of his head, and to all appearance could not live. Our beds had to be made down in the tent and were fixed comfortable. For the sick boy, all our family did all they could for him....He had by this time become unconscious. Mr. Rich came to my bed and called to me and wanted to know if I could watch over the boy awhile, for he must have a little rest. So, I got up and went to the bedside of the sick boy....[It was] thought the boy could not possibly live many hours. So, I took my seat beside the poor sick boy and began to reason with myself.

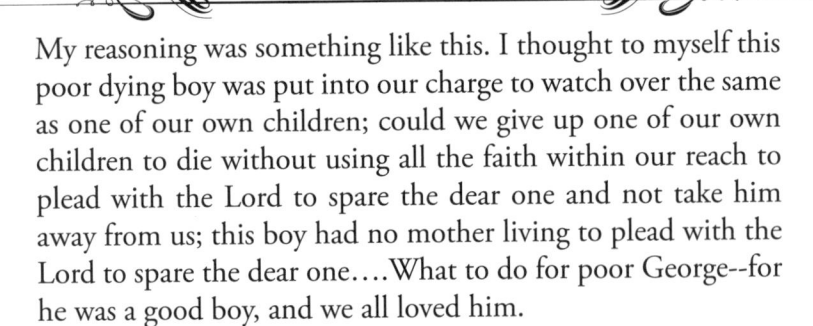

My reasoning was something like this. I thought to myself this poor dying boy was put into our charge to watch over the same as one of our own children; could we give up one of our own children to die without using all the faith within our reach to plead with the Lord to spare the dear one and not take him away from us; this boy had no mother living to plead with the Lord to spare the dear one....What to do for poor George--for he was a good boy, and we all loved him.

So when I got up from praying, I was led by my feelings to put a teaspoonful of consecrated oil in his mouth; his tongue was drawn far back in his mouth and was very black, and his breathing rattling and heavy, and his eyes to all appearance set in his head. I did not see that he swallowed the oil, so I anointed his face and head with the oil, asking the Lord to bless the same; then, in a little while gave him another teaspoonful of oil, asking the Lord at the same time with a humble heart to spare the boy and accept of my feeble efforts in his behalf. I felt broken-hearted before the Lord, and to my great joy, I noticed that George opened his eyes and looked upon me as though he was astonished. I said, 'George do you know me?' He spoke in a whisper, 'Yes.' Oh, how glad I felt by this time.

Mr. Rich had woken up and inquired how the boy was, saying afterwards that he almost feared he was gone. I said to him, come and see; the boy looked at him and smiled which astonished Mr. Rich so much that he turned to me and said, 'What has caused such a change?' I said to him, prayer and faith and hope in our Father in Heaven. I told my husband what I had done and how humble I felt while praying to the Lord to spare the boy's life. My husband was truly affected and told me the boy's life would be spared to yet be a blessing to me in some future time. And from that time on the dear boy continued to mend slowly and got well."

In later years, the promise of Apostle Charles C. Rich came to pass. George Patten grew to be a man, settled in Payson, Utah, married, raised a family and prospered.

Sarah wrote, "Many has been the time that [George] would bring me loads of provisions— butter and groceries when Mr. Rich would be off on missions to forward the work of the Lord. And when George would help me, he would always say 'Mam,' for that is what he calls me, he would say, 'Mam, I owe my life to you, for your faith and prayers saved me from death.'"

I am reminded, my dear friends, in this time when so many are shut in and suffering, that which we send out comes back to us again. It is the old axiom "cast your bread upon the waters and it shall be returned."

Source:

Autobiography of Sarah De Armon Pea Rich,

https://www.familysearch.org/tree/person/memories/KWJR-JBT

Claudius Victor Spencer

CHAPTER TWENTY-EIGHT

Storm on the Golconda

In January 1853, some four hundred members of the Church of Jesus Christ of Latter-day Saints were sailing from England to Zion. At one point in the Caribbean, the ship, The Golconda (a sailing ship), was calmed due to a lack of wind. To ease the boredom the saints gathered on the quarter deck for a dance. Among them, 29 year-old Claudius Victor Spencer, was among them. He was returning from service as a missionary in Europe. He records the following in his diary.

It was a warm sunshiny day, and we were a very merry party, but in the midst of our merriment a restless, gloomy foreboding influence took strong hold of me so much so that I left the party and went by myself and asked the Lord to tell me what it meant, and if it was not a warning, to take the feeling away, but it increased, after a little season I lifted my hat and said "Father in Heaven, if trouble is imminent, let peace come to me when I state to the captain to take in sail." I had not taken five steps until I knew I was going right. I found the captain sitting by the helmsman and told him, "I wanted him to excuse a cowardly landlubber and take in some sail." He jumped to his feet and asked, "Who's running this ship, him or me?" I answered "You're running the ship, but I am looking after the people." He got his speaking trumpet, hollered to the mate in the fore-castle, "Crack up two more sails... quick." At that time we had over two hundred Saints on the main deck, some singing, some sewing, enjoying themselves the best they could and a large number of us dancers on the quarter deck. There was not wind enough to fill a sail, not a cloud to intimate a storm when the captain gave the order to the mate. I told those around me to get below the deck "as quick as you can, there's trouble coming." They all started except Mrs. Hannah T. King— a strong minded woman, new in the work, not used to preemptory orders— I had to personally press her to move. She was the last one to go and her feet were on the bottom step of the stairs when the first mast fell, just grazing her head: in the meantime, I had jumped from the quarter-deck and run to the mid-ships, and ordered every man, woman and child to wait for nothing, but get below in a hurry. In ten minutes, every mast was torn out of the ship. We had been struck by a spent hurricane, off from the islands, without any earthly warning. If our people had remained above deck it would have been a terrible scene of suffering.... The next morning when I met the captain, he had tears streaming from his eyes. He asked, "What does this mean?" I told him, "It meant God was gathering Israel in the last days and sent his servants with them to care for them." He said, "Mr. Spencer, you can run this ship to New Orleans." And he used to come regularly day by day and ask me if everything was right, or if I had any suggestion to make.

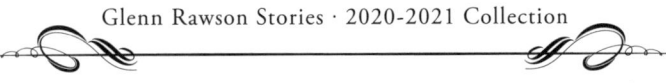

Source:

Diary of Claudius Victor Spencer. https://www.familysearch.org/tree/person/memories/KWJ8-WYB

Glenn, Dawni Jo, and Annie

CHAPTER TWENTY-NINE

Frary Peak New Years

If there are any of you out there wondering, after what you've been through with 2020, "How are we going to handle 2021, this new year?" Well, this is a lesson that my two lovely daughters, Annie and Dawni Jo showed me. Here's the story.

George Isaac Frary was born in 1854 in Wisconsin territory. In 1879, he married Alice Elizabeth Phillips. It is said that George was an experienced sailor on the Great Lakes. In time, he and Alice joined The Church of Jesus Christ of Latter-day Saints and after coming through Colorado, they moved to Utah. This was in the early 1890's. Around that same time when they arrived here, it was thought by some that Antelope Island was rich in mineral wealth, gold, silver, and later on oil and other things like that.

George and Alice decided to move out onto Antelope Island with, at that time, their four children and establish a claim and start prospecting. They knew what that island was like. They knew it was, deservedly, called a desert island and that life would be difficult. I can see George going, but Alice and the four children, they went, too. The Frarys built a three-room log cabin on Antelope island on the east side of the island, about south central. It was there that they raised their family. Life on that island was at best, a lonely, hard-scrabble existence. When the prospecting didn't pan out as hoped, they turned to ranching. At one time, George and John Dooley were the men instrumental in the introduction of the first buffalo on Antelope Island. The herd that is there now are remnants of those original ones brought out there by George Frary. On the homefront, it is said that Alice was an experienced teacher and taught her children in a home filled with love, music, and books. They would take whatever books they could get, and Alice had a small pump organ that filled that home.

On September 21, 1897, two months after the birth of their daughter, Florence Hope Frary, Alice became ill. George got into a boat and set out across the Salt Lake to get medicine and help around Ogden, or somewhere along the Wasatch Front. Accounts vary as to where he went exactly or what happened, but all agree that Alice passed away before George could get back to her. Her dying request to her children was to be buried on the island. Today a stone monument marks her grave on the island's east side. She was only thirty-eight years old.

The family left the island in 1902, but fanciful imaginations say that if you stand by Alice's lonely wilderness grave on a calm day you can hear the strains of her small pump organ carrying on the breeze.

Part 2 of the story:

On January 1, 2021, I set out with two of my beloved daughters, Dawni Jo and Annie (the youngest) to climb Frary Peak, which is named for the Frary family and lies immediately to the west of their homestead. Frary Peak is, as far as I know, the highest point on Antelope Island. We left in the mid-morning with sub-freezing temperatures. We walked 4.1 miles up the ridge and across the range to reach the top of Frary Peak and climbed 2500 feet in elevation. From the top we could see the Frary Homestead site down below us, though not very well. A weather system set in and obscured most of the valley in beautiful rolling fog. The fog and the clouds obscured most of the Wasatch Range, except for moments when the peaks, snow covered and glistening, would rise above the fog. The fog came up over Antelope Island's summit and moved on out across the lake. At one point on the summit there was only one small patch of blue sky and clear water in 360 degrees, and that was to the North. It was gorgeous!

Well, we took pictures, did the Instagram thing, etc. We were off the mountain in good time, celebrating our victory. Why did we go at such an unlikely time of the year? My daughter Annie expressed it for all three of us. She said, "I want to start 2021 on top of a mountain!" Just the way she said that, Jo and I said, "Amen sister! We are there!" And so we did. After all that all of us have been through in 2020, I hope that we are as tough and resourceful as George and Alice Frary, that we can stand the wildernesses of affliction and difficulty, and that we have, by the grace of God and hard work, many victories small and large in 2021.

Source:

https://www.familysearch.org/tree/person/memories/27S4-J66

https://www.deseret.com/1999/10/29/19472863/homestead-family-left-lasting-legacy-on-island

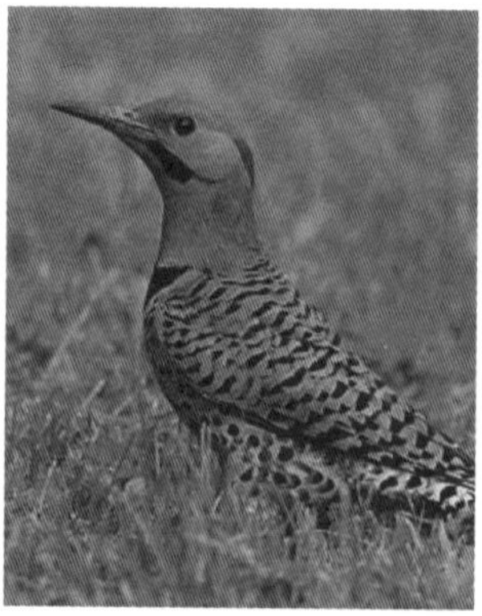

CHAPTER THIRTY

The Crazy Flicker

A day or two ago, I was standing in my kitchen looking to the south through the sliding glass door. Right outside, I noticed a bird just a few feet away on the edge of the grass, very close to the house. It caught my attention because first of all, it was a big beautiful bird, and second, because it was acting really, really weird.

The tinted glass door prevented it from seeing me, but I could see it clearly, so I moved closer and I stood watching it.

Its bill was about 2 inches long, pointed, and he kept poking it into the ground almost all the way to his eyes. It would thrust the bill in, pull it out, and do it again and again. He did it so fast I wondered to myself, "What in the world is this bird doing?" Every so often, it would shove his bill into the ground, give its head a twist, and flip as it poked its bill into the ground. Dirt and debris would go flying. I was so captivated watching it. The entire time was probably several minutes. I stood there watching it while it hopped around my lawn exhibiting this strange behavior.

"Is it feeding?" I thought. "But if it is, how can it know what's down there in the frozen ground?" On and on that bird went, poking holes in my lawn like a feathered aerator. Finally, it flew off and I stood there musing at its curious behavior.

His antics kept bothering me. Why? Finally, I got on the computer and looked him up. It turns out that the bird was a Northern Flicker—a species of woodpecker. I learned that he is one of the few woodpeckers that feeds on the ground as well as in the trees. In fact, it is said that up to 45% of its diet can come from ants and their larva which it digs out of the ground with its bill. Moreover, the article said that the flicker's tongue can project up to two inches off the end of his bill in the capture of prey. It has often been observed pecking at the ground the way other woodpeckers peck at trees.

That was it! My friend the flicker was feeding. It was lunchtime right outside my kitchen. Right where he was pecking the ground is where huge colonies of ants lived last summer.

When I first saw that bird, it made absolutely no sense at all. Its erratic actions seemed to lack all judgement and reason. It just looked…well…crazy. But it turned out, I was the one who was misjudging. The Flicker knew exactly what it was doing and was doing that which nature had programmed it to do for itswinter survival and sustenance. Smart bird!

We are like that flicker. As Christians, we do things every day of our lives that make no sense to the people of the world that are watching us. In fact, we are weird! We are often criticized, persecuted because of what we think, what we feel, and what we do makes no sense whatsoever to the world who does not share our values. We try to live moral lives in an immoral world. We believe in kindness and civility in the midst of a society of vicious incivility. We reverence our bodies as heavenly gifts while those around us see it as a mere toy to be decorated and played with, and on and on we could go.

Make no mistake about it, we make no more sense to the people of this world than that crazy flicker made to me. They think we are crazy. Well—you're not. They just don't see yet what drives you. But mark my words, they will, and those who have mocked, scorned, and persecuted will rue the day they ever did.

Source:

https://en.wikipedia.org/wiki/Northern_flicker

Lorenzo Dow Barnes

CHAPTER THIRTY - ONE

The Forgotten Missionary

We speak sometimes of those who waste and wear out their lives for the Lord Jesus Christ's sake. Let me tell you of one man whom history has forgotten.

Lorenzo Dow Barnes was born in 1812 in Tolland, Massachusetts, the son of Phineas, a New England farmer. He was named for Lorenzo Dow, the great evangelist. In 1815, Lorenzo's family moved to Ohio, where in 1833, young Lorenzo was taught the gospel and baptized. Immediately after his baptism, he went out as a missionary. When the Lord called for volunteers to march with Zion's Camp to redeem Zion in Missouri in 1834, Lorenzo volunteered. Upon his return, in the summer of 1834, Lorenzo was among the first seventies called in this dispensation, in early 1835.

Again, no sooner was he ordained a seventy than he set out again as a missionary. It is said that the 23-year-old missionary had limited education and a speech impediment. He stuttered, which caused enemies of the Church to single him out for attack. Evidently though, Lorenzo had some spine. He did not back down or run away, and engaged in numerous debates with opposing clergymen. Not only did those debates ultimately yield baptisms, but Lorenzo overcame his weakness and became a powerful orator.

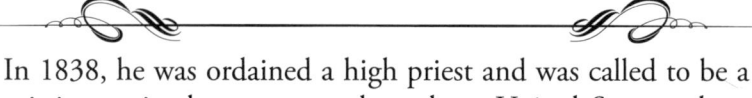

In 1838, he was ordained a high priest and was called to be a missionary in the eastern and southern United States, where he traveled without purse or script and established several branches of the Church, in Pennsylvania and in the South.

Then in 1841, Elder Barnes led a company of saints to Nauvoo where he courted and married Susan Conrad. He'd only been married a short time when he was again called to serve as a missionary. This time, the call was to England. It was while serving as president of the Bradford Conference that Elder Lorenzo Barnes passed away. He was thirty years-old. It was said of him that he was "possessed of most untiring perseverance, industry, and application and wore out his life by constant preaching and exposure." After his death, the local saints, led by Elder Wilford Woodruff, took up a collection and erected a stone memorial over his grave in Idle, Yorkshire. It reads:

> *In memory of Lorenzo D. Barnes, who died on the 20th of December 1842, age 30 years. He was a native of the United States, an Elder in The Church of Jesus Christ of Latter-day Saints, a member of the High Priests Quorum and also of Zion's Camp in the year 1834, and the first gospel messenger who has found a grave in a foreign land.*

Lorenzo Barnes was the first missionary of The Church of Jesus Christ of Latter-day Saints to give his life while serving on foreign soil. He would not be the last. He left behind a wife, no children, and an undeniable legacy.

Source:

https://familypedia.wikia.org/wiki/Lorenzo_Dow_Barnes_(1812-1842)

https://www.familysearch.org/tree/person/memories/KWVW-YF2

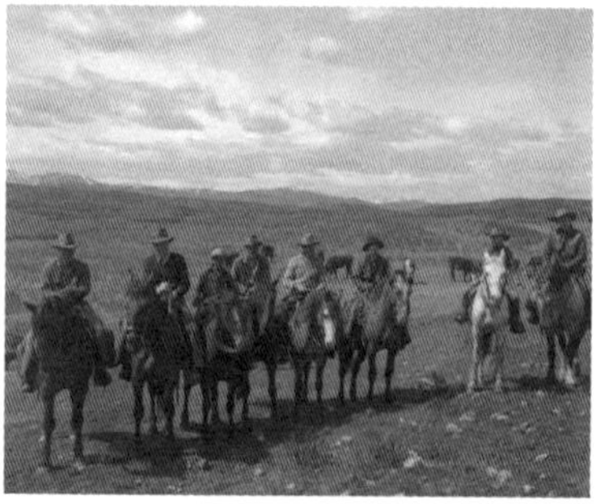

CHAPTER THIRTY - TWO

Mothering Up!

I remember as a boy growing up on a ranch in southeastern Idaho, in the Lemhi Valley area. In fact, at this time we were living in Leadore. Every year, the people my dad worked for would round up their herds and drive them to summer pastures up near Gilmore. Every year we had this ritual where we would drive the cattle up to the summer pastures, and it was for this boy, an exciting time so much so that I never minded always being the one appointed to bring up the rear and eat the dust. I remember one drive in particular where we didn't reach the home pastures until shortly after dark. This was at the end of the summer when we were bringing them down from Gilmore back to the ranch at Leadore. Well, we got to the pastures and it was after dark. Tired, worn out, ready for a rest, I headed for the barn. But my dad asked me to stay behind and watch the herd.

I protested, "Why? I want to go home. There are fences. They're not going to go anywhere."

Well, my dad explained that the cows and their calves had become separated during the drive. By instinct, he said, they would return to the last place they had seen each other in an effort to "mother-up" as he called it. It would be necessary for me and others to stay behind, ride the fence, and keep them in the pasture until all the cows found their calves. Well, at the time, other than being a little ticked off that I couldn't go home, I didn't think at the time it'd be that big of a deal. It was dark. Surely they would bed right down.

Oh, I was wrong – very wrong! I remember clearly to this day running my horse blindly back and forth in the dark, along that fence, trying to keep those cows and calves in. They were so determined that even at the smallest hole in the fence, they would stick their head in it, and they'd plow right on through. It was a scary, grueling night, and years later it became a powerful learning experience. You see, nature endowed a familial bond between those cows and calves. A very strong bond, so much so that they would fight their way through any obstacle to get to each other. And the noise – the noise of an entire herd, cows and calves, calling to each other – well, it was loud.

Over the years, I've thought a lot about that experience. I don't think it's a whole lot different with people. We are the children of God. He is our Father – literally. We have a Father and a Mother in Heaven. Contrary to what is taught in schools today, we are not accidents of nature – some end of the evolutionary chain gang, some kind of half-breed monkey. No, God is part of us, and we of Him. The gene pool originates with Him, and He has planted within each of us a homing instinct, – a drive if you will, that yearns for Him and for our Heavenly home, for the peace, the happiness, the joy, and the love we once enjoyed in His presence. And yes, He is calling us. Those who will honestly soften their hearts and listen will hear and feel that Heavenly tug. And if we doggedly persist each day in calling back to Him, and breaching every fence that gets in our way, there will come a day, a blessed, beautiful day of joy for which we all hope, when He will welcome us home with open arms.

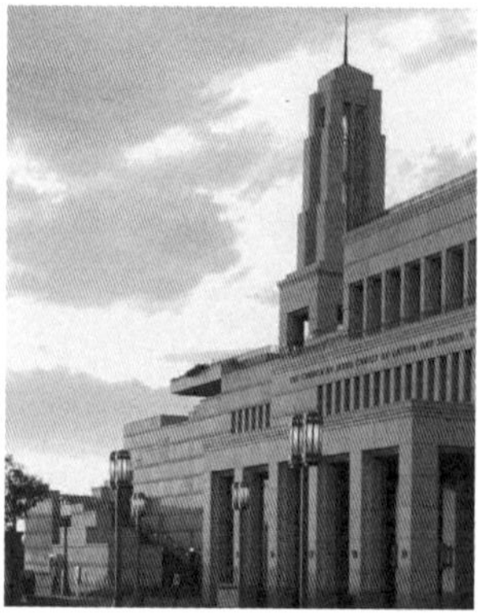

CHAPTER THIRTY - THREE

He Was So Kind and Nice

Kim Moss shared this story with me. He was there and he was the witness. He tells the story of a time when he was serving as a host and tour guide on Temple Square in Salt Lake City. He was giving a man a tour of the Conference Center. As they approached the fountain area on the plaza level, right where you look up to the highest levels of the building, the man Kim was guiding said, "Excuse me, may I tell you a story?"

"Absolutely." Brother Moss said.

"I am not a member of your faith," the man said. "I am from North Carolina, but I helped with the construction of this building. Right here in this spot where the fountain is, we had scaffolding set up that went all the way to the ceiling. The scaffolding was wrapped with a green tarp on all four sides, all the way from the top, down to the last level where there was a slit in the tarp about 8 feet off the ground. We [would] go up and down the scaffolding a dozen times a day and we were pretty good at it. I could come down from 100 feet in the air to ground level in just a few seconds. On this particular day I was coming down swinging on the bars like a monkey, flying down from level to level. I popped out the slit in the green tarp, hit the ground, and the next thing I knew I was face down, spread eagle on the tile floor. I heard a voice behind me saying, 'Boys, Boys let him up.' As I was released, I rolled over on my back, looking into the face of the kindest old man, holding a cane, bent over with his arm stretched out saying, 'Here, I'm Gordon, let me help you up, these boys get a little excited sometimes.' He was so kind and nice as we visited, I will never forget him."

The kind, old man was President Gordon B. Hinckley. He and his security detail just happened to be touring the Conference Center, which Kim said President Hinckley often called his "baby," on a quiet day during construction and they just happened to be walking by the scaffolding when the man popped out of the curtain directly in front of President Hinckley. The highly trained security men reacted immediately to the perceived threat and took him down. President Hinckley instantly read the situation and with characteristic humor and kindness, rescued the poor worker.

I will never forget President Hinckley either. Of all the prophets I've ever known, he was so down to earth and spoke so directly to me. I love him. I miss him.

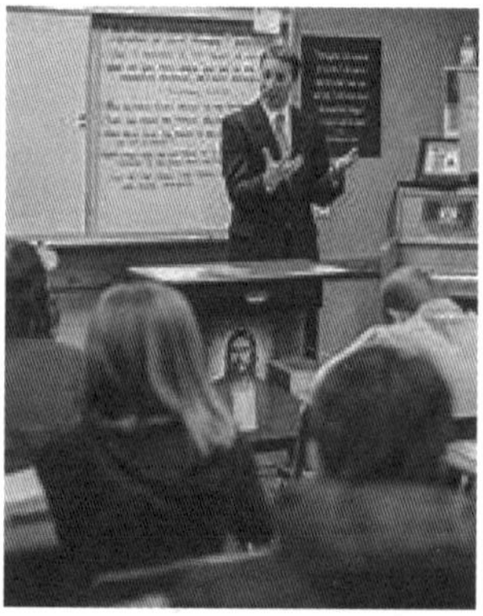

CHAPTER THIRTY - FOUR

Can You See What I Just Did to You

My friend, Lynn Kenley, shared this with me. He's an old Seminary teacher, retired now. He used to teach at Granger High School. Perhaps some of you had him as a student. He shared this wonderful story with a powerful point. He tells me, "Sometimes it was a struggle to get the students in seminary to do an entire devotional." I know because I was there and went through it, too. So when one of Brother Kenley's students at Granger High School asked to do the whole devotional, he was overjoyed. But then, the young man said, "I will be using a guitar." "Okay," Brother Kenley said. "I will be using an electric guitar," he explained. "Okaaay!" Brother Kenley said. "And it will be amplified," the boy concluded. "Ohhh!" said Brother Kenley, "How loud?" "**Loud!**" he said.

Brother Kenley gave him the go-ahead. That familiar voice said, "let him do it." His next thought was that he should probably warn the other teachers. Brother Kenley explains what followed.

The day of the devotional came. He had everything set up and ready to go. I stood in the back of my classroom waiting. His first song was so beautiful I thought I was going to cry and, as I looked around the room, I saw others completely involved. His second song was a bit more animated and there was a lot of toe tapping going on in the room with a ton of smiles. Then came the third song- a really loud head banger that about brought bricks out of the wall. I was even jerking my head in time with the music. All of a sudden, he turned that amplified sound into dead silence about half-way through the song. Students who had been almost bouncing out of their desks were almost angrily hollering for him to keep going. Quietly, he turned, put his guitar away and turned to the class and said, "Can you see what I just did to you with music in a few short minutes? What can Satan do to us with music if we aren't very careful?" He quietly sat down in his desk to a very quiet and pensive room full of students--which included me.

This boy well understood the power of music and entertainment. As President Nelson recently said, "Each time we resist entertainment or ideologies that celebrate covenant-breaking, we are exercising faith in Him, which in turn increases our faith." (General Conference October 2020, Embrace the Future With Faith.) So much of what is today called entertainment is covenant breaking. It is powerful, subtle, persuasive, and if we are not careful, deadly.

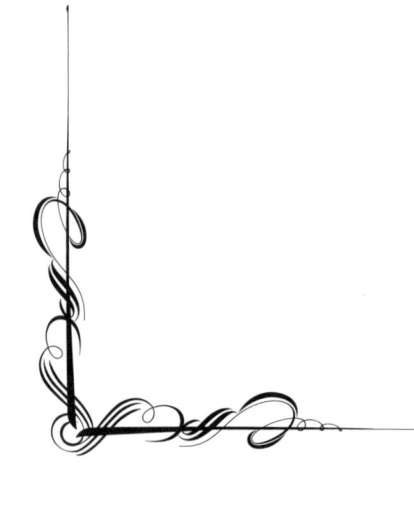

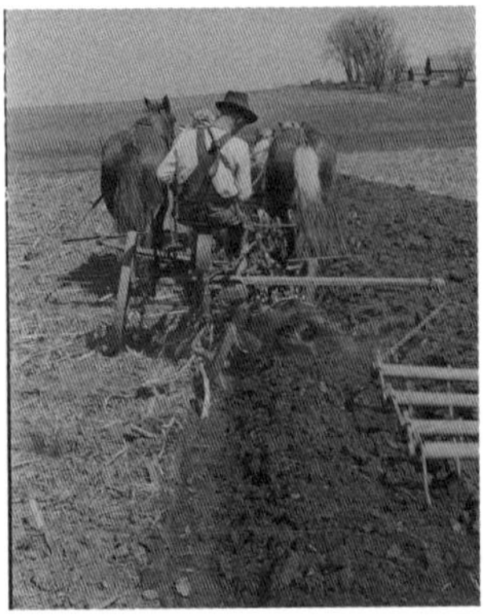

CHAPTER THIRTY - FIVE

The Team Would Not Move

Llewellyn Mantle was born in South Wales in the year 1808. He grew up learning the trade of a wagoner— someone who built wagons. On June 2, 1835, Llewellyn married Katherine Watkins of Herefordshire, England. In 1842, Elder George Allen of The Church of Jesus Christ of Latter-day Saints taught the Mantles the gospel and baptized them. Shortly after that, the Mantles sold all they had and set out for Zion. They arrived in Nauvoo in early 1844, where they became acquainted with the Prophet Joseph Smith. Family history records the following of their association with the Prophet.

> *"Llewellyn worked on the Nauvoo temple and was a member of the Nauvoo Legion. They lived in one of the Prophet's houses and worked on one of his farms. Llewellyn was an excellent horseman and teamster."*

One early summer day, Llewelyn was out on the Prophet's farm plowing with one of the Prophet's teams when something unusual happened.

> *"Suddenly, the team stopped, hanging their heads, and refused to go on. This was very unusual, for the team was very dependable. Nothing could persuade these horses to move. So, he let them stand until they wanted to go on working again."*

It was a most unusual event. Llewellyn would later learn that the moment this happened was just after 5:00pm on June 27, 1844, the very time of the Prophet's martyrdom.

Source:

https://www.familysearch.org/tree/person/memories/KWJ8-SHS

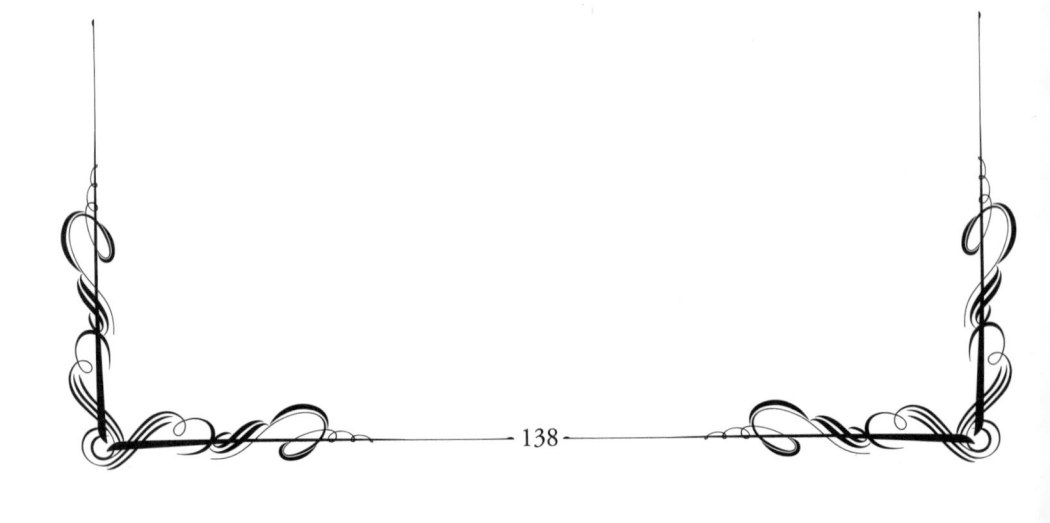

Stockings

CHAPTER THIRTY - SIX

The Wanderer

I remember when I was just a little boy. I grew up on a ranch in Hayden Creek Valley in the Lemhi Valley, central Idaho. When I was just a boy, I came home from school one Spring day, and as was my habit, I called my dog, Stockings, he was waiting for me, and off we went to explore. Living on a ranch in a remote part of Idaho provided plenty of wilderness for that opportunity. I loved to wander through the trees, along the creeks, and over the hillsides. I loved it then and I still do.

The problem on this particular day was that I lost track of time. When I realized it was getting dark, I was miles from home in my wandering. I knew I couldn't make it back before it was too dark to see my way, and where I grew up, there was no such thing as street lights or signs, or even traffic. There was nobody. It was mountain country. I looked around me and saw that I was closer to a neighboring ranch farther up the mountain than I was to my own house. So, I set out for their place, arriving just after dark. When I explained my situation to them and asked them to take me home, they didn't seem all that interested. They said they would, but they moved slower than molasses on a winter night and it got later and later, darker and darker.

I kept thinking, "I'm in trouble, I am so dead. My dad is going to tan my hide." Time dragged on, and my fear increased. It was a dark, moonless, cold night and I was scared, nearly in a panic. Then I saw headlights coming up the rutted road.

As the truck approached, it was my dad. I wasn't sure I was saved or dead, but the look on his face quickly gave me to understand that it was probably more the latter. He didn't yell at me, He just pointed back down the dark mountain road and said, "Start walking."

I thought he must be joking. He wasn't. Terrified, I walked a few hundred yards down that dark, lonely road and then finally overwhelmed, sat down by the side of the road, my arms wrapped around my dog and began to cry. My dad pulled up a few minutes later, threw open the door and told me to get in. I climbed into the warm pickup and he took me home. Strangely, he didn't say a word on that drive down the mountain. He didn't have to. I thought I knew what I had done wrong, but as it turned out, I had no clue.

We walked into the house. The lights were dim, and my mother was sitting in a front room chair right by the door, crying like I had never seen her cry. When she saw me walk through the door, she came out of the chair with a sob and threw her arms around me and cried with relief. She thought her little boy had wandered off and fallen into the flooding, spring runoff creek behind the ranch and drowned. I will never forget that night and the pain and worry on my mother's face. It cut so deep and hurt so much. I vowed never to do that again to my mother. I couldn't bear it. My dad quietly allowed me to learn that hurting my mother was one of the worst things I could ever, ever do. I never forgot it. To this day, my mother and I are the best of friends.

I speak to all of you who have wandered. Do you have any idea of the worry and pain you are causing those who love you? Probably not, because if you did, you wouldn't do it. Come home. Come back to heart, home, and heaven while you still can.

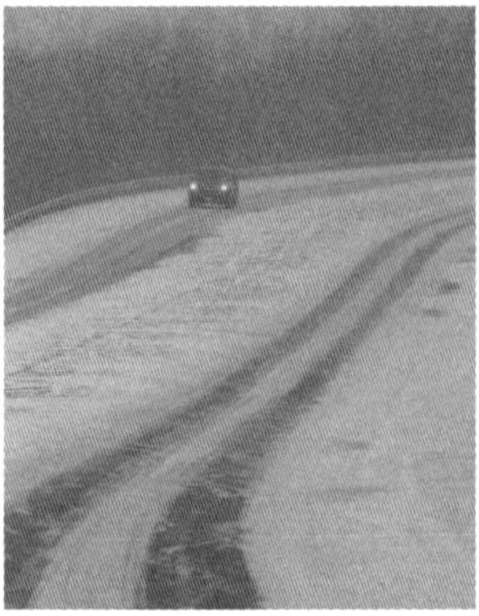

CHAPTER THIRTY - SEVEN

Daddy, I'm Scared

One winter night, it was very late and I was tired. My cell phone rang. It was one of our daughters. The moment I heard her voice, I knew something was wrong.

"Daddy," she barely managed to say, "I'm scared."

"What's wrong," I asked.

She explained that she was on the interstate highway trying to get home and had driven headlong into a terrible blizzard. It was very dark, and the snow was coming down so hard that the lines on the highway were obliterated, as were the marker posts on the side of the road. She was driving blind and terrified.

"I'm scared," she repeated, amidst her sobs. "What do I do?"

I have been in that situation many times and I understood her fear. My heart and soul went out to her. I would have come and got her in a moment if I hadn't been 200 miles away.

"Okay," I said, "This is what you do," and then I explained all the tricks I have ever learned as a professional driver on how to drive and stay alive in a blizzard; how to stay on a road you can't see. Even as I was explaining this to her, a large truck came out of nowhere, obscuring in an instant what remaining vision Hannah had. She was so scared at that moment, she cried out in terror.

As we talked, she became calmer. Though she was still crying and still scared, she felt she could make it. We closed the call and I prayed for her.

She made it home.

My dear Hannah reminded me of a powerful lesson. Don't forget when you are in trouble and things are out of control that there is someone always there and always listening—who can see you and help you, and knows what you need. All you have to do is cry out,

"Father, I'm scared. Help me."

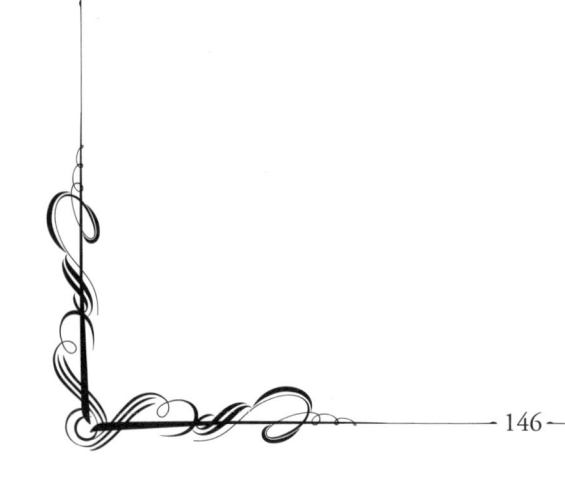

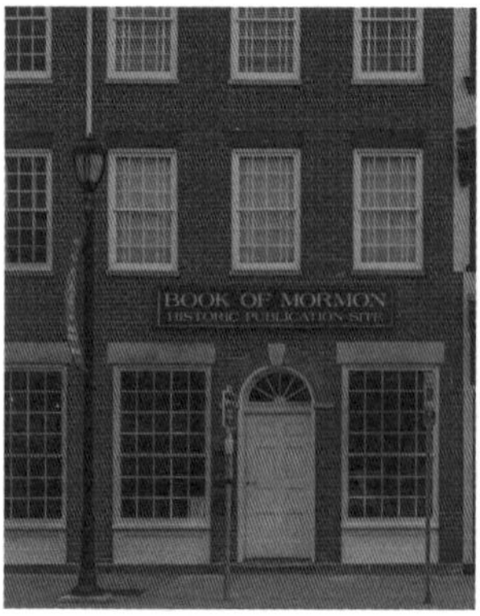
BOOK OF MORMON
HISTORIC PUBLICATION SITE

CHAPTER THIRTY - EIGHT

March 26, 1830

Someday in the future when we are beyond this life and can look back on this mortality from the vantage point of eternity.... when we are able to see our history as God sees it, there will be certain events and dates of greater significance than the world ever knew. They will be those moments, like the birth and resurrection of Christ, largely unnoticed, that will have done the most good, for the most people, for the longest time. Among those dates will surely be March 26, 1830. That date signaled the beginning of a marvelous work that would sweep the entire earth and affect every nation, every people, indeed every family.

God himself marked that moment as a sign to all the world that a great work would commence among all people where he would gather out from all the nations of the earth the scattered and lost members of the tribes of Israel, and restore them to their respective lands of inheritance.

That moment was also a stern warning to all the world. "When ye shall see these sayings coming forth among you, then ye need not any longer spurn at the doings of the Lord, for the sword of his justice is in his right hand, and behold at that day, if ye shall spurn at his doings he will cause that it shall soon overtake you" (3 Nephi 29:4).

What was this event that God marked as a sign of a great change coming? What happened on March 26, 1830?

It was on that date in a small, two-story brick building in Palmyra, New York that the Book of Mormon first went on sale.

The Book of Mormon—a marvelous work and a wonder, a witness and a warning.

Source:

2 Nephi 30:3-8, 3 Nephi 21, 30

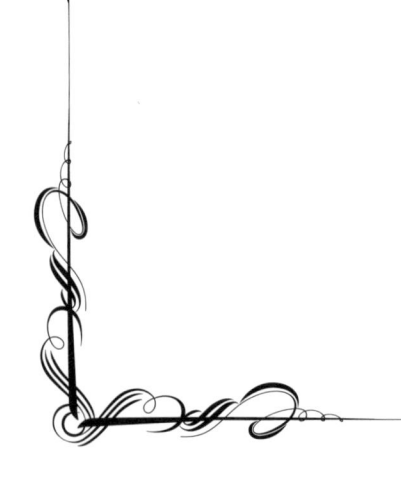

Hannah and Shaina

CHAPTER THIRTY - NINE

The Power of iPod

Our family traveled to visit relatives in another state. We were about an hour into our trip when I heard a commotion in the back seat. I looked into the rear-view mirror and witnessed a most comical sight. There were our two teenage daughters, Hannah and Shaina, with a single iPod between them and sharing the earphones. Hannah had an earbud in her right ear and Shaina had the other one in her left ear. The funny sight was this skinny little cord connecting the brains of my two girls. It was as close to two people sharing a brain as I have ever seen. Even funnier was what they were doing. No one else in the car could hear what they could hear, and yet, there they were singing at the top of their lungs, or as loud as I would let them, and they were doing it in perfect unison.

I kept watching. It amazed me how much in sync, how much "one" these two actually were, and not just with their singing. One minute, they were singing the exact same words in perfect unison, and the next, they were laughing in unison. Then there was the annoying percussion as they pounded on my back seat, again in rhythm, even with hand and body actions. All this gyration going on in the back seat, and it was in perfect unity with two girls sharing a brain with an iPod. They entertained themselves for well over an hour this way. With over 400 songs to choose from on their iPod, they could have gone on until virtual exhaustion.

These two girls, Hannah and Shaina, especially at that time, were very different. They had nearly opposite tastes in music, movies at that time, boys, and other such vital things for teenage girls, and yet by the power of iPod, they were one. As I watched them, I thought to myself, if only there was a way we could hook everyone in this world up to the same iPod so that we all shared the same brain to bring individuals, families, nations, and the worlds into such a perfect harmony. If only there was a way to connect the brains and hearts of all men so that they would think as one, feel as one, act as one, and be one.

But there is! What is that power that connects all men and makes them one in heart, mind, and soul? It is the power of the Holy Ghost. Across peoples, cultures, languages, and race, the Lord is always the same. His message is always the same, and always He brings men into unity and harmony with each other and with God if they will let Him. Two people filled with the Spirit of God cannot long remain two in mind and heart. They must become one if they are meek and lowly of heart and willing.

We worship the Father, in the name of the Son, by the power of the Holy Ghost. What is more important today in your schedule, or tomorrow's schedule, than qualifying yourselves for the gift of the Holy Ghost, the power of His presence,

and the power to be one with Him and those around you?

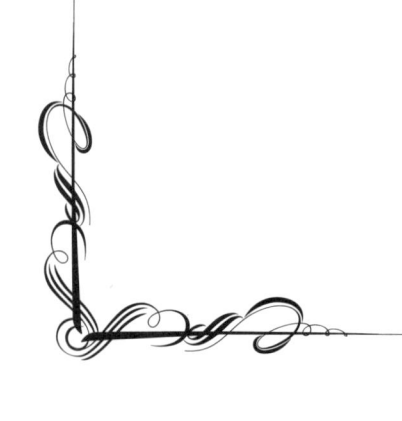

Wilford Woodruff

CHAPTER FORTY

Living Oracles

President Nelson's teachings the last six months have been for me like a lifeline to a drowning man. His words and his teachings have been as powerful and comforting to me as the Book of Mormon itself. Thank the Almighty for President Nelson, the prophet of God. I know he is a prophet. In that regard, the following story comes from the journal of Wilford Woodruff, and is dated sometime around January 1842, when this happened.

It was at a meeting in the home of the Prophet Joseph Smith, the Old Homestead, (there in Nauvoo down by the river, not the Mansion House, but the Old Homestead.) It was while Joseph was living there that a meeting was held. Hyrum, Joseph's brother, was called on to teach. He stood by the dormant fireplace and preached on the importance of the scriptures. "We must take them as our guide alone," Hyrum is quoted as saying.

Years later, President Wilford Woodruff, in the 1897 General Conference, expanded on the essence of what Hyrum taught that day. He quoted Hyrum as saying, "You have got the word of God before you here in the Bible, Book of Mormon, and Doctrine and Covenants; you have the written word of God, and you who receive these revelations should give heed to what is in those books, as what is written in those books is the word of God. We should confine ourselves to them."

He had laid down the Bible, the Book of Mormon and the Doctrine and Covenants.

According to President Woodruff's earlier diary account of the matter, Joseph then turned to Brother Brigham, who at that time was the President of the Quorum of the Twelve Apostles to speak next. Brigham would say, "I had become pretty well charged with plenty of powder and ball....I felt like a thousand lions." President Young stood up, took each of the books of scripture, piled them on top of each other, and said, "I would not give the ashes of a rye straw for all those books for my salvation without the living oracles. I should follow and obey the living oracles for my salvation instead of anything else."

According to President Woodruff, when Brother Brigham finished, Brother Joseph said to the congregation: "Brother Brigham has told you the word of the Lord, and he has told you the truth." (President Wilford Woodruff, Conference Report, October 1897, Afternoon Session.)

The aftermath of that, no one ever tells this part of the story, but it's so powerful. Hyrum had been soundly and publicly corrected, if not rebuked. According to President Young's later account, "Hyrum arose and made a handsome apology, and confessed his wrong which he had committed in his excess of zeal, and asked pardon."

Source:

Hyrum Smith A Life of Integrity Jeffrey O'Driscoll, p. 250-251

The Great Salt Lake Shorelands Preserve

CHAPTER FORTY - ONE

Something is Going On - The Gathering

It was most unusual. I was sitting at my desk when an idea came into my mind- "Go to the Salt Lake Shorelands Preserve." I jumped in my truck, and I headed south, and got out there just as the sun dropped below the western horizon. I arrived at the Preserve, wondering why I was there. I parked my truck facing west to watch the last colors of the sunset. After a few minutes, I noticed there were a lot of crows flying directly over my head headed west, from the Wasatch Mountains out towards the lake. Then I noticed there were a lot of crows. I stepped out of my truck and looked. There were crows for as far as I could see both east and west—hundreds of them, maybe thousands of them. They just kept coming and coming. I got out my camera and filmed them. I've never seen anything like it. If a flock of crows is called a "murder," then this was "mass murder." They flew straight toward the setting sun, not as one big, huge flock but as a long line that kept coming. I wondered how long they would keep coming. Finally, the last bird came. He was just a little, bitty fellow far behind but flapping for all he was worth. "I'm coming, Dad! Wait for me!" Off they went.

I stood there musing at the strange event. It probably makes perfect sense to an ornithologist, but I'm not an ornithologist and I was baffled. Had all the crows from Salt Lake City to Brigham City hit the end of their workday and were now on their long commute home to roost for the night? Was it sort of a crow rush hour? Was there something else, a weather or feeding pattern, that was causing this? The bottom line—I had no idea. I determined to go back the next night and see if it happened again. Sure enough, same spot, same time, right at 5:30p.m., a lone crow flew over headed west. I looked east and here they came, thousands of them flying just like they had the night before. For 15 minutes, crows flew over me bound for some destination in the west. As the last crow passed, I started my truck and took off west following them. About 3 miles later, I came close enough to their flight path that I could see them off in the distance. As I studied them through the binoculars, one huge group flew off to the west out over the lake when I lost sight of them. Another group seemed to be right down, just above the ground circling, some landing, some rising. They did this for some time, then all at once, the whole bunch of them lifted off, lined out, and flew out after the others. I saw this strange circling, hovering pattern twice. It appeared that some of the birds would tire from the long flight and would land to rest while the rest of the flock, the "murder," tightened up and circled overhead in a tight pattern. When all were sufficiently rested, they flew off to join the others for the roosting grounds for the night.

While I pondered and wondered what all this meant, Connie Henrie, found an article and sent it to me which quoted bird expert Bridget Butler, who called herself a crow diva, explained. She says:

> *Crows are very social creatures and at this time of year they often flock together by the thousands for warmth, safety, and, possibly, convivial conversation....As we move into the wintertime - it generally starts in November and goes through March – crows start to roost together in very, very large numbers. And we can see hundreds, up to thousands.... During the wintertime, crows kind of need each other. During the summer they're hanging out in small family groups [of] two to eight crows. And then in the wintertime it's really beneficial for all these birds to*

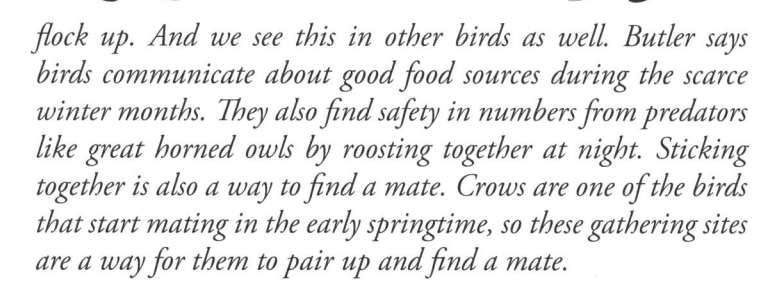

flock up. And we see this in other birds as well. Butler says birds communicate about good food sources during the scarce winter months. They also find safety in numbers from predators like great horned owls by roosting together at night. Sticking together is also a way to find a mate. Crows are one of the birds that start mating in the early springtime, so these gathering sites are a way for them to pair up and find a mate.

It appears that crows gather together in the most difficult of times in the year for warmth, strength in numbers, safety, mutual support, and social interaction.

In the October 2020 General Conference, President Russell M. Nelson said of the latter-day gathering of Israel, "For centuries, prophets have foretold this gathering, and it is happening right now! As an essential prelude to the Second Coming of the Lord, it is the most important work in the world!" When we are baptized and sealed in the temple as covenant families, whether on this side of the veil or that, we are fully gathered. And why do we gather? Why have we gathered ever since 1830? For the exact same reasons the crows do. The Lord said this of the gathering to take place just before the Second Coming.

> *And it shall come to pass among the wicked that every man that will not take his sword against his neighbor must needs flee unto Zion for safety. And there shall be gathered unto it out of every nation under heaven; and it shall be the only people that shall not be at war one with another. And it shall be said among the wicked: let us not go up to battle against Zion, for the inhabitants of Zion are terrible; wherefore we cannot stand. (See DC 45:68-70)*

The part that touched me the most about the crows is when one of the young or old would tire and land, the stronger ones appeared to come together and circle overhead protecting the weaker ones until they were sufficiently rested and ready to go on and then all went together. The little guy struggling to keep up was not left behind. Can we learn a lesson from the crows?

Source:

https://www.vpr.org/post/something-crow-about-flocks-gather-thousands?fbclid=IwAR08iwFLwZxcGYTnge2koBLPE6c88QCSjsGj-YScqa3JQaIs-vPgOvA5p8s#stream/0

Adam

Chapter Forty-Two

Adam's Dream

Some years ago, our family was gathered around on a Sunday night taking turns sharing something we had learned. We heard everything from the profound to the silly. Then it came for nine-year-old Adam, and he told us of something he had learned when he was about six.

It was during family scripture study. A verse was read that told Adam that if you do something wrong, you should pray to Heavenly Father, and He would come down and touch you. The lesson stuck with him. Not long after that, Adam experienced a dream. In the dream, he had done something very wrong, and he felt horrible. And then he saw a bright light. It was the Savior. He came down and spoke to Adam, telling him that if he would go and say he was sorry, he could feel better. Jesus then stretched forth His hand and touched my little boy. He said the touch made him very happy and made him feel as though he could do this. He then went to his little sister and said he was sorry. As he did, he described that he felt good. He felt righteous and sin-free from that moment forward. Over the next week, the dream came back to him again and again, and each time it did, he said he felt good about repenting.

I asked him what he learned from the dream, and my wise, little man said, "If you repent, you can always feel good about yourself."

And he's right.

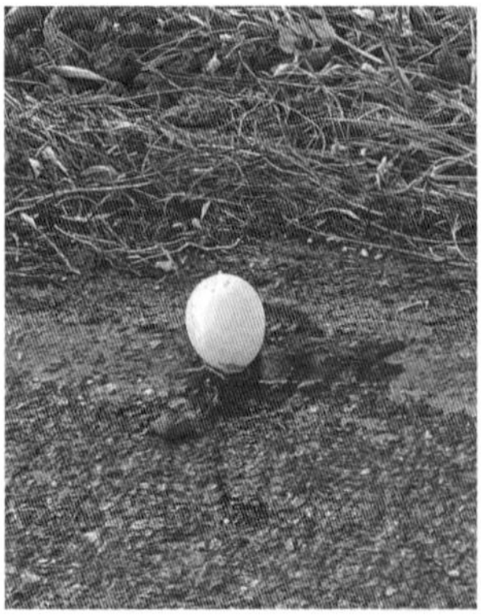

CHAPTER FORTY - THREE

The Egg on the Highway

I woke up this morning and just as the sun was coming up, I went out to run. As I sometimes do, while I was out running, I was listening to a conference talk on my airpods. It was a talk given in 2017 by Elder Dallin H. Oaks, where Elder Oaks talked about the meaning in the scriptures of the term "the world." Elder Oaks went on to caution us to stand apart from the "slow stain" of the world. He defined what the world was and then said "Don't live after the manner of the world." In short, the world is not our home. We came from a better place to prove ourselves and go back. While we are here, in mortality, we are to stand and live in holy places apart from wickedness. I had just finished the talk and was running along a country street when I came upon a most unusual sight.

Right there on the side of the road, just on the edge of the asphalt, was a chicken egg—that's right—a chicken egg. It wasn't smashed. It was an intact chicken egg on the edge of the pavement. I gave it a glance as I was running and went right on past it. Then something said, "Whoa, slow down, boy, and go back and look at that. You don't see that every day." So I stopped. I turned around and went back and looked at the chicken egg. How in the world did a chicken egg all intact wind up on the asphalt on the highway? Then I noticed that on one end it had a tiny little crack and some of the contents of the egg had leaked out. I looked around, trying to figure out how that chicken egg had gotten there. I noticed that just to the right of the road was a ditch, a culvert, and a bridge, and a big netwire fence. On the other side of the fence was a whole flock of chickens with a very proud rooster strutting among them. The fence between the road and the chickens was a broad weave netwire fence that any chicken could walk through in a moment. It appeared that a hen had walked through the fence and up on the edge of the road and left her gift right there on the asphalt.

I took some pictures and went on with my run, knowing I had seen something significant, but not sure what it was. So I kept running. Then it hit me.

We are like that egg. We are children of Almighty God—divinity in embryo we are, living in a fallen world that is not of our true nature. The majority of the people of this world are on the fast track to hell and suffering and self-destruction. If they do not repent they will be at least damaged and at worst outright destroyed just as surely as that egg is not going to last. We no more belong with the people of this world on that road than that delicate chicken egg belongs on the highway. Just as that egg should be safely nested and nurtured where it belongs, so too, we should keep ourselves safely nested on the covenant path, gathered under the wings of the Master. It is where we belong!

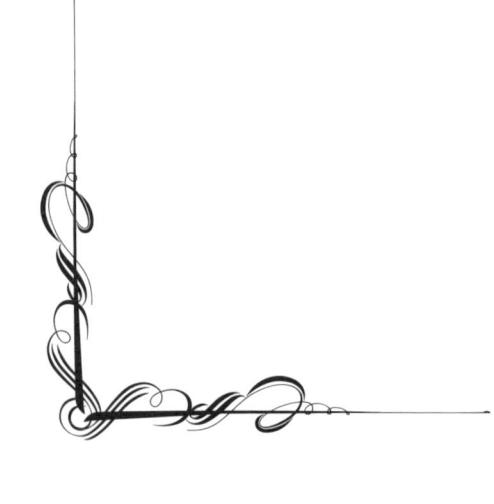

Amasa Mason Lyman

CHAPTER FORTY - FOUR

Amasa Mason Lyman

How far will the Lord's mercies reach for the repentant? I think you and I would be shocked if we knew.

Two missionaries came into the small New Hampshire community of Lyman. Living there was young Amasa Mason Lyman, 19 years old, who had been searching earnestly for the truth. Upon hearing the sure testimonies of Elders Orson Pratt and Lyman E. Johnson, he was converted and baptized on April 27, 1832. He was immediately rejected by his family. He determined to join the saints in Ohio some 700 miles away—his greatest desire being to meet Joseph Smith. It was July 1, 1832, when Amasa Mason Lyman first met Joseph Smith, the Prophet. As they shook hands for the first time, Amasa later recalled, "I felt as one of old in the presence of the Lord. My strength seemed to be gone, so that it required an effort on my part to stand on my feet…and the still, small voice of the Spirit whispered its testimony in the depths of my soul, where it has ever remained that he, Joseph Smith, was a man of God."

Shortly after that, Amasa was called as a missionary—again and again and again he was called, serving ten missions in ten years. He was a member of Zion's Camp, and later one of those standing with Joseph when a Missouri militia general ordered them all to be taken to the public square and shot the next morning. After much devoted service, Amasa was called as an apostle and, in Nauvoo, as a counselor to the

Prophet Joseph Smith. Upon Joseph's death, it was Amasa who stood with Brigham Young and the Twelve, instead of his fellow counselor Sidney Rigdon, and influenced all the saints to follow Brigham and the Twelve.

Amasa was a full participant in the events of the Great Mormon Exodus of Nauvoo in 1846, and the subsequent colonization of the west. He did so much, for so many, for so long. Then in the 1860's, there began to be problems. Inexplicably, the man who had been so valiant and devoted so much of his time and life, began to teach strange doctrines, and manifest an attitude of rebellion. His brethren, and the Twelve, were patient and attempted reconciliation, but finally when Amasa stubbornly would not relent and would not repent, he was excommunicated from the Church in 1870. He died February 4, 1877 in Fillmore, Utah, not a member of the Church- An apostle who became an apostate.

As we mortals tend to judge matters, that's a terrible story with a tragic ending. Amasa's story was a terrible tragedy. He had done so much good, and after all of that virtually to stumble at the finish line— If it ended there, it would be a terrible story.

However, the story does not end there. There is more. Sometime in 1908, one of Amasa's daughters experienced a dream in which she saw her father, dressed in black, and standing across the wide gulf of a river. Martha tried to go to him, but she could not. He told her he was tired of wearing black, that he missed his family, and then he said, "Go tell Francis. He's the only one who can help me." Francis was Amasa's son and the president of the Quorum of the Twelve Apostles.

When Martha's dream was related to Church President Joseph F. Smith, he said, "It sounds to me like your father has suffered long enough. We'll see what we can do."

Subsequently, on January 12, 1909, Francis Marion Lyman was baptized by proxy on behalf of his father, and President

Joseph F. Smith laid his hands upon him and confirmed him a member of the Church and restored all of Amasa's former blessings—his priesthood, his apostleship, his sealings.

It was Elder Orson F. Whitney who wrote, "Though some of the sheep may wander, the eye of the Shepherd is upon them, and sooner or later they will feel the tentacles of Divine Providence reaching out after them and drawing them back to the fold. Either in this life or the life to come, they will return. They will have to pay their debt to justice; they will suffer for their sins; and may tread a thorny path; but if it leads them at last, like the penitent Prodigal, to a loving and forgiving father's heart and home, the painful experience will not have been in vain."

Source:

Amasa Mason Lyman: A Labor of Love, by History of the Saints, 2013

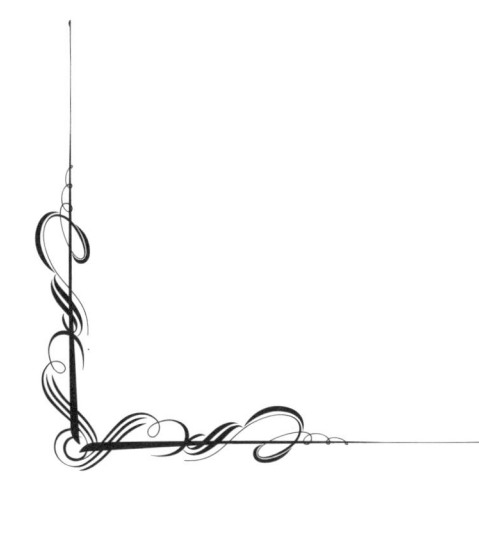

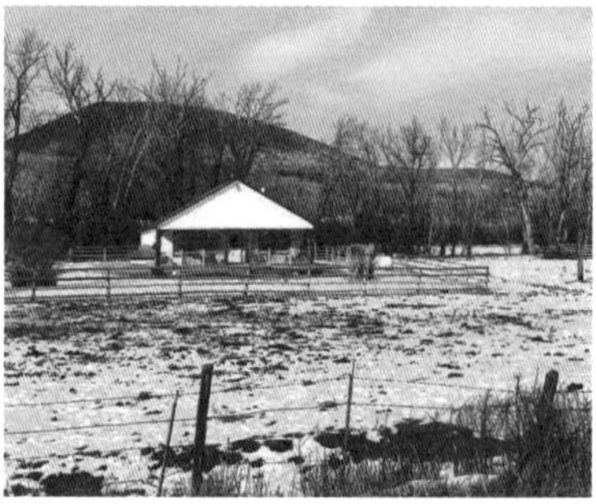

CHAPTER FORTY - FIVE

Chores

If I had known what I was getting into, I never, never, never would have asked. I was about five-years-old. We lived on a ranch in the Lemhi Valley of Idaho, Hayden Creek. My dad bought a Guernsey milk cow and named her Buttercup. Every night and morning after Buttercup calved, dad would go out to milk her and that milk was good! To this day, there is nothing as good as home-milked milk. I would go out with him and I would watch. I can still picture that barn in my mind. I can still see my dad sitting there milking a cow and squirting it into the cat's mouth, even squirting it at me. I watched him do this and I thought "that looks like great fun!" I asked him if I could try it.

He finally said I could. That first milking of the cow turned into a twice a day chore for the rest of the years I lived at home. I quickly tired of it, but dad insisted, "No, that's your job now." And on it went from there. In addition, and in time, it was added to the milking, feed the stock, water the stock, do this, do that—every night—and every morning—rain or shine—hot or cold—no matter my school or sports schedule— I had chores to do, and dad made sure of it. We would come in from a long day in the saddle and dad would make sure we took care of the horses before we took care of ourselves. No matter that we worked in the fields from daylight to dark, we still had to be up early and out late to get the chores done. Those chores were like a religion to him and he held me to it, until I finally left home. I remember one night, long after dark, going out to milk the cow in a driving blizzard. I couldn't find her. I stumbled through the snow and wind, colder than a popsicle, until I finally found that cow and got the job done, because I knew my dad wouldn't let me quit.

I cannot tell you how much I hated those chores then and how grateful I am for them now. A chore is defined as "1. an ordinary job that must be done regularly or 2. an unpleasant, boring, or difficult thing that must be done." My chores were both.

A few weeks ago, I drove back up to the Valley and stopped by that old milk barn where it all started. It has since collapsed to the ground and is rotting away. It's gone, but what this child learned there, endures. I learned, through those chores, the value and importance of work, and being steadfast at it, and never giving up. Thanks be to God for an old-fashioned dad who gave me chores that contributed to the welfare of my family. I believe it made me a better man.

Please consider a broader application of chores. A chore is an ordinary, sometimes boring or unpleasant job or task, that must be done daily. Studies have shown that a number of benefits come to those who discipline themselves with daily "chores." May I suggest just one, one of many, significant chores that typifies many that, if done daily, will change our future forever. "Cry unto Him in your houses, yea, over all your household, both morning, mid-day, and evening" (Alma 34:21).

We have been given meaningful chores by the Almighty and asked to be diligent—which means to be attentively persistent in getting them done. How are we doing? How are you doing? Figuratively speaking about spiritual chores--are the cows still alive?

Source:

https://www.macmillandictionaryblog.com/chore

Maren Hansen Peterson

CHAPTER FORTY - SIX

Ole and Marn

Ole and Marn Peterson had left Denmark in April of 1857, bound for Utah. Once in America, they had been assigned to the Park handcart company. However, at the Missouri River, Marn, who had an infection in her leg, was told she would never make it to the valley. They stayed near Council Bluffs and farmed, preparing for that day when they could continue on to Zion. Then in the spring of 1861, a large wagon train was organized and Ole and Marn and their four children, Peder 14, Annie 6, and the babies, Mary and Joseph, joined with them.

Somewhere along the trail, sickness spread through the camp and little Annie became ill. Notwithstanding, she was administered to and the fervent prayers on her behalf, Annie grew weaker until at last she was declared dead. There was danger on the trail from Indians. Hence, it was decreed that the company could not linger with enough time to dig a proper grave. According to family records, the child was wrapped in a blanket and covered in heavy brush and the company went on.

Death was no stranger to Ole and Marn as they had already buried three children in their native Denmark. Nevertheless, it was hard to leave Annie behind under those circumstances. Obedient to their captain, they went on. They had not gone far when it was deemed expedient that they had to make camp as Indians threatened.

That night around the fire, as was customary, the company sang, "Come, Come Ye Saints," the great anthem of the trail. As the company raised their voices "all is well, all is well!" the feeling gnawed at Marn that all was not well. It was like the Spirit was trying to tell her something.

"Ole," she said, "I can't feel our baby was dead."

"I know, dear," said Ole gently. "We had so many plans, but she was, and there is nothing we can do now but pray that we will be able to raise the family we have, and more when we settle in Zion. Come to the wagon so you will be refreshed for tomorrow's travel." Wearily Marn started for the wagon.

"Ole, listen to the wolves, and our baby is lying back there alone, not even protected by a grave. How can we stand to go on?"

"We must make up our minds to go on and trust in the Lord for the rest," he replied.

"I can't, Ole! I just can't!" Gently but firmly, Ole took her by the arm and led her back to their wagon.

The next morning at dawn, Ole discovered that Marn was not in her bed and nowhere to be found in the camp. A search was mounted until suddenly someone spotted her in the distance coming toward camp from the east. She was carrying a burden and stumbling with weariness.

Ole ran to his wife and lifted the burden from her arms. As he spoke to Marn, it struck him that the burden was Annie—and the child was warm—she was alive.

Annie Christina Peterson would recover and live to marry Samuel Wilcox, bear nine children, and as a midwife bring many children safely into mortality. God be thanked for his inspiration and for all those mothers who can hear it, who in love and tenderness listen and never give up on us.

Source:

Donald Long History at https://familysearch.org/photos/stories/2875272

https://www.familysearch.org/tree/person/memories/KWJJ-VXY

Dimick Huntington

CHAPTER FORTY - SEVEN

Joseph and Emma, The Reunion

March 20, 1839, in the dank, cold, dungeon cell of Liberty Jail in Clay County, Missouri, Joseph Smith and four other companions were imprisoned. By the duplicity of traitors, they had been arrested and on the strength of testimony offered by false friends, they had been confined in the close quarters of the darkened dungeon since December 1, 1838. Nearly four awful, lonely months over the cold winter, Joseph and his companions had endured terrible privations and humiliation within the forbidding stone walls of Liberty Jail.

They were judicial hostages, held in bonds by the Missourians, to ensure that the Latter-day Saints left the state. Agonizingly helpless, they languished on a rough stone floor, as their friends and families were mobbed and driven from the state.

"Oh, God, where art thou," Joseph dictated on this date, "and where is the pavilion that covereth thy hiding place? How long shall thy hand be stayed, and thine eye, yea, thy pure eye, behold from the eternal heavens the wrongs of thy people and of thy servants, and thine ear be penetrated with their cries?"

For almost twenty pages—Joseph poured out his soul in a letter that has no equal in Church History. From that letter would come not only a revealing view into the noble soul of Joseph Smith, but also, later, three revelations of the Doctrine and Covenants. That letter is on many levels, a documentary treasure.

At the very end of the letter, Joseph himself penned a note to his wife Emma whom he had not seen for so long. Among other things he said,

"Never give up on an old tried friend, who has waded through all manner of toil for your sake, and throw him away because fools may tell you he has some faults."

Joseph was a sensitive man and indeed cared what people thought of him. Where were his friends at this gloomy, awful hour? Did they now brand him a criminal and consider him of no worth? And more importantly, did Emma?

Two weeks later, on April 4, 1839, Joseph wrote another short note to Emma, and after pouring out his affections for her and the children, he wrote again,

"I feel like Joseph in Egypt, doth my friends yet live? If they live, do they remember me—have they regard for me? If so, let me know it in time of trouble. Dear Emma, do you think that my being cast into prison by the mob renders me less worthy of your friendship—no, I do not think so."

Moroni once told Joseph that his name would be had for good and evil, and of the many things of his ministry most difficult, those friends who turned against him cut the deepest.

In late April 1839, Joseph was now a free man, and struggled in his gaunt, weakened condition to reach Emma. He had to have wondered as he walked across the Missouri prairie going east, "Will Emma welcome me?"

Dimick Huntington, sent by Emma, went down to the Quincy, Illinois boat landing looking—waiting—inquiring for news from Missouri when he saw a disheveled stranger leaning against a fence rail. His ragged pants were tucked into old boots full of holes. His hat pulled down over his face to hide his identity, yet something was familiar. Dimick approached him, looked into his face and exclaimed, "My God, Brother Joseph, is that you?"

Recognizing his old friend, Joseph insisted that he be taken immediately to his family. Dimick located a second horse and together they rode the three miles out east of Quincy where Emma was staying. As they approached the house of the Cleveland's, Dimick reigned in his horse and held back while Joseph dismounted and turned toward the house. Suddenly the front door burst open, and Emma ran out and threw herself into Joseph's arms before he was halfway to the gate. His questions were answered. Welcome home, Joseph.

Source:

Rough Stone Rolling by Richard Bushman p. 381-82

The Quincy Miracle: A Rescue Never To Be Forgotten by History of the Saints, p. 80-82

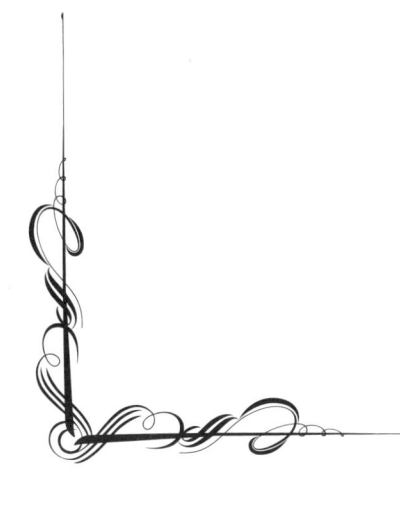

William Bradbury

CHAPTER FORTY - EIGHT

The Blind Carver

One day in 1842, a visiting Congregational minister, Thomas Salmon, paid a visit to a friend where he lived in Coleshill, Warwickshire, England. Salmon described the visit as follows:

I became acquainted with W. W. Walford, the blind preacher, a man of obscure birth and connections and no education, but of strong mind and most retentive memory.

In the pulpit, he never failed to select a lesson well adapted to his subject, giving chapter and verse with unerring precision and scarcely ever misplacing a word in his repetition of the Psalms, every part of the New Testament, the prophecies, and some of the histories, so as to have the reputation of knowing the whole Bible by heart.

He actually sat in the chimney corner, employing his mind in composing a sermon or two for Sabbath delivery, and his hands in cutting, shaping and polishing bones for shoehorns and other little useful implements. At intervals, he attempted poetry.

On one occasion, paying him a visit, he repeated two or three pieces which he had composed, and having no friend at home to commit them to paper, he had laid them up in the storehouse within.

How will this do? asked he, as he repeated the following lines, with a complacent smile touched with some light lines of fear lest he subject himself to criticism.

I rapidly copied the lines with my pencil, as he uttered them.

Reverend Salmon left England in 1842 and returned to the United States. In 1845, Salmon submitted an article for the newspaper, The New York Observer, in which he offered the poem composed by William Walford, with this tentative proviso, "if you should think them worthy of preservation."

The editors felt the tender poem worthy of inclusion and published it on September 13, 1845. About fifteen years later ,the great composer William Batchelder Bradbury set the poem to music. The lovely and touching hymn gained slowly in renown until it was finally published for the first time in 1878 in a Methodist hymnal.

After the hymn was established in the hearts of Christians everywhere, scholars and students went back to England to find William Walford, the blind poet. They never found him. He remains a mystery yet unsolved to this day. We cannot say for certain who he was or be even the least bit familiar with him, yet the poem he wrote bespeaks a man familiar with His God and the power and intimacy of personal prayer. Walford wrote,

Sweet hour of prayer, sweet hour of prayer

That calls me from a world of care and

Bids me at my Father's throne,

Make all my wants and wishes known.

In seasons of distress and grief

My soul has often found relief

And oft escaped the tempter's snare

By thy return, sweet hour of prayer

Source:

https://dianaleaghmatthews.com/sweet-hour-prayer/#.YH3sfqlKjX0

https://sermonwriter.com/hymn-stories/sweet-hour-prayer/

https://hymnary.org/person/Walford_WW

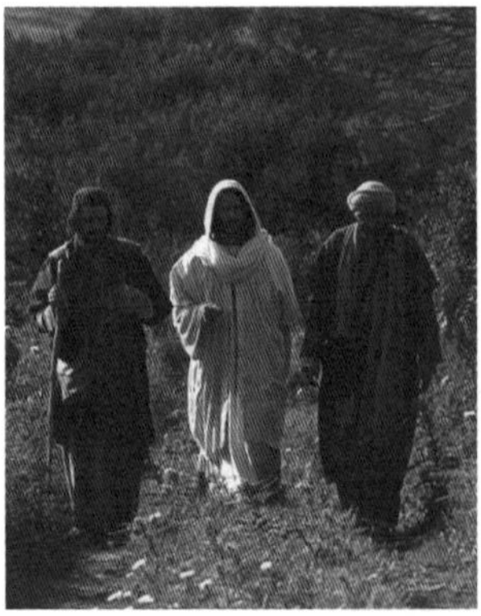

CHAPTER FORTY - NINE

The Stranger on the Road

Just after Peter and John had come, at Mary's bidding, to the empty Garden Tomb, two disciples left Jerusalem for the village of Emmaus about 7-8 miles distant. Not only does no one know for certain exactly what village is Emmaus in that country now, but little to nothing is known for certainty of who these disciples were; only one was named—Cleopas. It is assumed that the other one was Luke, but we don't know.

As the two men walked, "they communed together and reasoned." A stranger drew near to them and asked "what manner of communications are these which ye have one with another, as ye walk and are sad? And one of them, whose name was Cleopas, answering said unto him, 'Art thou a stranger in Jerusalem, and hast not known the things which are come to pass there in these days.' And he said unto them, 'What things?'"

The two disciples then told him Jesus of Nazareth, "a prophet mighty in deed and word before God and all the people." They then told him how the chief priests had condemned Jesus and delivered Him over to be crucified. They revealed the source of their grief and sadness. "But we trusted that it had been He who should have redeemed Israel." Do you see what they are saying? They were going through a faith crisis. Their faith was shaken, and their hearts were grieved and troubled by rumors of angels and reports that he was alive, when they, with their mortal understanding, knew assuredly that He could not be alive. At that point, the stranger said to them,

"O, fools and slow of heart to believe all that the prophets have spoken. Ought not Christ to have suffered these things and to enter His glory?" The stranger then opened up the scriptures and taught the words of the holy prophets concerning the mission and ministry of the Messiah. As He did, their hearts burned within them" and they knew the truth of His words, and the power of that man.

This conversation must have lasted for miles because about this time, they approached the village of Emmaus. It was towards evening and the stranger made as though to journey on, but the two disciples said, "Abide with us; for it is toward evening, and the day is far spent."

The mysterious stranger accepted their gracious invitation for hospitality, lodging and food. "And it came to pass, as he sat at meat with them, he took bread, and blessed, and brake, and gave to them. And their eyes were opened, and they knew Him; and He was taken up out of their sight." It was Jesus, their Lord and Master. He was, indeed, alive. It was Him all along, but their eyes were "covered that they could not know Him."

This story does attest that a resurrected being can eat and drink and hide his identity and look like a normal man. This story may mean many things, but to me it means at least this. Cleopas and his companion invited a stranger to abide with them and receive their hospitality, and in so doing, the Lord came to them and gave them so much more than they gave him. Remember what the Lord said, "Inasmuch as ye have done it unto one of the least of these my brethren, ye have done it unto me." What if they had turned the stranger away? What if they had just let Him go on his way?

Could it be that each time we literally or figuratively invite a stranger close to abide with us and receive our love, our comfort and kindness, it is He who at the end of the day comes to abide and we who receive the greater comfort and love.

And that is an experience we can't wait to tell the whole world about.

Source:

JST Luke 24

Charles Gabriel

CHAPTER FIFTY

The Plowboy Composer

It is remarkable what the Lord can do with someone who has faith and is willing to use the talents they are given.

Charles Hutchinson Gabriel was born in 1856, one of seven children born to an Iowa farmer, Isaac Newton. and Cleopatra Cotton Gabriel were his parents. In addition to farming near Sugar Creek, Iowa, Charles' father taught singing schools. Charles was about 10 years of age before he ever saw his first musical instrument, which was a rough type of harpsichord. Later on, came a piano.

From a young age, Charles showed a talent and a love for music. At the age of 15, he made up his mind and announced to his mother that he wanted to be a songwriter. While working in the fields on the family farm, Charles would compose melodies in his mind and then write them down in the evening. One story suggested his musical talent was recognized, even as a lad, in his boyhood hometown. The pastor of the local church which his family attended saw Gabriel walking in town early in the week and asked him if he knew a good song to go along with the sermon topic for Sunday. By the end of the week, young Gabriel had written a song for that Sunday with words and music.

When Charles was only sixteen, his father passed away and the following year, he began to travel and lead his own singing schools. He later found employment teaching music in Texas and Oklahoma schools, worked at Grace Episcopal

Methodist Church in San Francisco, and then for a publishing firm in Chicago.

It is said that Charles' loved to sing and wrote songs every day. Over the course of his life, it is believed that the prolific composer wrote over 8,000 songs, mostly hymns. "During his life he edited 35 gospel song books, eight Sunday School song books, 10 children's song books, and countless other music collections including anthems, cantatas, and instructional books." Not only was the man prolific in his compositions, but demonstrated a powerful understanding of and love for the Lord and the scriptures.

Charles Hutchinson Gabriel earned a unique legacy among American hymn writers. His contemporaries called him the "Prince of American Hymn Writers"—And all of this from a man who never had a music lesson in his life. This master of sacred music was taught his craft by the grace of God.

In 1898, he penned the words and wrote the music for this great Christian hymn,

I stand all amazed at the love Jesus offers me,

Confused at the grace that so fully he proffers me.

I tremble to know that for me he was crucified,

That for me, a sinner, he suffered, he bled and died.

Oh, it is wonderful that he should care for

Enough to die for me!

Oh, it is wonderful, wonderful to me!

Charles Gabriel is a living legacy and testament to the very thing he wrote about—that the love and grace of the Savior will raise all of us, if we are willing, from humble obscurity to exalted royalty.

Thank the Lord for the plowboy composer who became a prophet of music.

Source:

https://archive.is/20130121190548/http://desmoinesregister.com/apps/pbcs.dll/article?AID=/99999999/FAMOUSIOWANS/501300335

https://www.thetabernaclechoir.org/articles/i-stand-all-amazed---video-and-lyrics.html

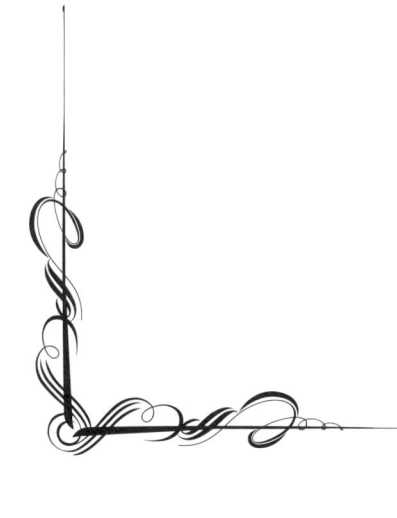

James Talmage

Chapter Fifty-One

Lord, If Thou Wilt

In the time of the Savior, leprosy was a terrible, incurable disease. Elder James E. Talmage said, "Leprosy was nothing short of a living death, a corrupting of all the humors, a poisoning of the very springs of life; a dissolution little by little, of the whole body, so that one limb after another actually decayed and fell away." Moreover, the curse of leprosy went beyond the physical torment. The person so afflicted was considered unclean under the law of Moses and required to separate themselves from all human contact. They were cast out and cut off from home, family, friends, and all love and association, and consigned to live in the ruins or tombs with only the company of others similarly cursed to die slowly. Scarcely could there be a more miserable, disgusting way to live, suffer, and slowly die in pieces than leprosy.

Somewhere in Galilee, early in the Master's ministry, a man full of leprosy approached the Savior, and fell before him, worshipping him.

"Lord," he cried, "if thou wilt, thou canst make me clean."

The man knew the Messiah had the power to heal him, but would he? Would he take pity on one so unworthy, so loathsome, and despised?

Mark records, "And Jesus moved with compassion, put forth His hand, and touched Him, and saith unto him, 'I will. Be thou clean.'"

What a sight it must have been, for immediately, the leprosy fell away and the man was made whole before their very eyes. Can you imagine the man's gratitude?

Jesus straitly commanded the man to tell no one but go to the priests and present the offering required by the Law of Moses. Jesus had made him whole; the priests would pronounce him clean and bring him back into the community.

Please consider—what if that leper, in a manner of speaking, represents every single one of us in our fallen, unrepented state— our sins as the misery thereof and its loathsome effects slowly killing all of us spiritually. But then, we learn of Jesus and we come to Him knowing full well that we are unworthy, sick, and afflicted spiritually before Him and we ask for His help. When no one else can or will help us—He will! No matter who or what, or how bad off we may be, it is required of all of us to ask for His help. When we do, like that leper bold enough to ask, Jesus will reach across all distances and with His healing hand—touch us and heal us no matter now loathsome the disease, the sins.

Source:

James E. Talmage, Jesus the Christ, p. 200-201

Mark 1:40-43

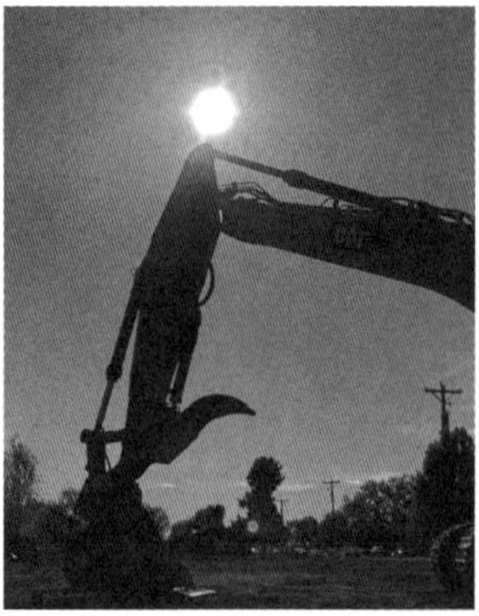

CHAPTER FIFTY - TWO

Gone in a Single Morning

Last night I saw it. I was coming home. A large Caterpillar trackhoe was parked very close, shutdown, and waiting at the back of the house. That thing was parked too close to be normal. I looked again, over my left shoulder, at the house. It was a beautiful two-story brick home, well-appointed with carefully landscaped grounds—it seemed a lovely home that anyone would be grateful to have. Well, I sort of put it out of my mind.

This morning, I woke up at about 5:00 a.m. and went out for a run, just about 20 minutes before sunrise. I didn't think about it, but about an hour into that run I was on my return leg coming home and happened to come right past that house. I turned the corner just in time to see the long boom and claw on the trackhoe reach up above the roof, out, and demolish the entire front section of that gorgeous home. The claws came down over the front entryway of the home, and it collapsed into the rubble that was the rest of the house under the tracks of that mechanical beast.

I stood there for a moment. I stopped running and watched. Then I kept going. I felt a strange, sad feeling. What a beautiful home! I imagined, in my mind, the family or families that might have lived, loved, and felt joy and made memories there—and now it was gone—both the home and the family. Gone. The potential joy and security of that home is no more.

I thought of the weeks, months, and even years that it had taken to build that home and create those beautiful grounds, and it was gone in a single, destructive morning. I later went back, this afternoon. All that was left was a hole and a pile of broken concrete. I know that it was necessary for the onward march of human progress. Those machines are marvelous; they are cool to watch. But to me, it still felt sad.

I reflected throughout the day how that home literally is like our homes figuratively. Evil destructive forces stand ready, waiting and watching. At the first opportunity, they attack, usually from behind when and where we least expect it, and in a single moment of choice can destroy a loving family that took decades to build. And all that is left in their wake is an emotional crater and the shattered rubble of human hearts.

President Nelson taught the women of the Church in October 2020 Conference, "As turmoil rages around us, we need to create places where we are safe, both physically and spiritually. When your home becomes a personal sanctuary of faith—where the Spirit resides—your home becomes the first line of defense."

And so, of course, where is it that the Evil One can maximize the most misery for the least effort—in our homes, the attack on our homes. Gone, all gone, in a single morning!

Source:

Russell M. Nelson October 2020 General Conference, General Women's Session https://www.churchofjesuschrist.org/study/general-conference/2020/10/37nelson?lang=eng

About The Author

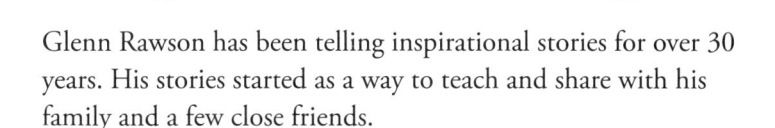

Glenn Rawson has been telling inspirational stories for over 30 years. His stories started as a way to teach and share with his family and a few close friends.

Glenn Rawson was born and raised in Idaho. He grew up on a cattle ranch, and to this day still carries a little bit of cowboy in him. When he was 18 years old, he joined The Church of Jesus Christ of Latter-day Saints and later served a mission in Iowa. He graduated from Brigham Young University with a degree in Wildlife and Range Science, and later from Idaho State University with a Master of Education degree. He spent almost 20 years as a seminary and institute teacher.

In 1997, he began writing and producing stories for the radio. His stories continue to be heard on numerous stations around the country. That work in radio later turned into production work for church specials. Then, in 2008, he joined with KJZZ television in Salt Lake City and the Joseph Smith Papers team to produce a weekly documentary television series entitled, The Joseph Smith Papers. In 2010, he teamed with Dennis Lyman and Bryant Bush to produce a new series called History of the Saints. Glenn and his wife Debbie have seven children and eighteen grandchildren. They live in Utah. Glenn is a simple storyteller whose goal is to inspire and lift people.

In addition to traveling around the world, he has studied the scriptures extensively and is happy to present this book to you.

For information about receiving weekly stories and other books available, please visit

glennrawsonstories.com or historyofthesaints.org.